Safeguarding Vulnerable Adults

A Training Package to Enhance Practice

Robert Adams

RHP

Russell House Publishing

This manual, first published in 2008, forms part of the *Safeguarding Vulnerable Adults* training package, which the author aims to keep up-to-date, communicating with you via the publisher. **Registering your purchase enables you to obtain – where appropriate:**
- **copying rights**
- **the electronic version**
- **notification of updates for use across your organisation**.
See the Preface for further details.

Russell House Publishing Ltd.
4 St. George's House
Uplyme Road
Lyme Regis
Dorset DT7 3LS

Tel: 01297-443948
Fax: 01297-442722
e-mail: help@russellhouse.co.uk
www.russellhouse.co.uk

British Library Cataloguing-in-publication Data:
A catalogue record for this book is available from the British Library.

ISBN: 978-1-905541-37-9

Typeset by TW Typesetting, Plymouth, Devon
Printed by Ashford Press, Southampton

About Russell House Publishing

Russell House Publishing aims to publish innovative and valuable materials to help managers, practitioners, trainers, educators and students.

Our full catalogue covers: social policy, working with young people, helping children and families, care of older people, social care, combating social exclusion, revitalising communities and working with offenders.

Full details can be found at www.russellhouse.co.uk and we are pleased to send out information to you by post. Our contact details are on this page.

We are always keen to receive feedback on publications and new ideas for future projects.

Contents

The *Safeguarding Vulnerable Adults* workbook

Updates, copying permission, and electronic supply of The *Safeguarding Vulnerable Adults* Workbook

Foreword

Robert Adams

This authoritative package is built around a workbook prepared by Denis Hart and provides practical guidance on how to use the law in work with adults who are vulnerable to abuse.

Whilst the *Human Rights Act 1998* affirms people's right to live free from abuse of all kinds, it was not until 2005 that the then Association of Directors of Social Services published a statement of standards for good practice in safeguarding adults (ADSS, 2005). This was the culmination of a growing weight of research evidence attesting to the significant and widespread problem of abuse of vulnerable adults in many different situations: visually impaired people (Action for Blind People, 2008), people with dementia (Alzheimer's Society, 1998), learning disabled people (Bailey, 1998), people in residential settings (Cloud, 1995) and older people (DoH, 1995; McCreadie, 1996). More recently, there has been research which brings together the evidence from different sectors (O'Keeffe, Hills, Doyle, McCreadie, Scholes, Constantine, Tinker, Manthorpe, Biggs and Erens, 2007).

The package is designed for work-based training and university-based teaching. It can be used as the basis for self-study, short courses, or as part of a longer educational sequence in adult safeguarding or work with adults. Its virtue is that it is accessible, accurate, up to date and practice-based guidance which will both inform and stimulate critical reflection.

References

Association of Directors of Social Services (ADSS) (2005) *Safeguarding Adults: A National Framework of Standards for Good Practice and Outcomes*, London: ADSS.

Action for Blind People (2008) *Report on Verbal and Physical Abuse towards Blind and Partially Sighted People across the UK*, London: Action for Blind People.

Bailey, G. (1998) *Action Against Abuse: Recognising and Preventing Abuse of People with Learning Disabilities*, London: ARC.

Clough, R. (1995) *Abuse in Residential Institutions*, London, Whiting and Birch.

Department of Health/Social Services Inspectorate (1995) *Abuse of Older People in Domestic Settings: A Report on two SSI Seminars*, London: DoH.

McCreadie, C. (1996) *Elder Abuse: Update on Research*, London: Age Concern, Institute of Gerontology, King's College.

O'Keeffe, M., Hills, A., Doyle, M., McCreadie, C., Scholes, S., Constantine, R., Tinker, A., Manthorpe, J., Biggs, S. and Erens, B. (2007) *UK Study of Abuse and Neglect of Older People (Prevalence Survey Report)*, London: NatCen.

Preface

This package of materials can be used across your organisation in the training and teaching of anyone who has, or who will have, contact with vulnerable adults. Offering affordable and updatable solutions for both small and larger organisations to copy it to all their learners, it can be used:

- With students in college or university.

- With practitioners, such as carers and social workers, as part of their training at work.

The *Safeguarding Vulnerable Adults* Workbook features:

- Key text for all workers with vulnerable adults

- Accessible guide to practice that makes the subject come alive

- Authoritative information on using the law and procedures

- Many practice examples to stimulate critical reflection

- Includes *Mental Capacity Act 2005*, *Safeguarding Vulnerable Groups Act 2006*, *Mental Health Act 2007* and **subsequent legislation** addressed in the updates

- Covers human rights, domestic violence and inter-professional work.

The **workbook has been designed so that students and practitioners** can either undertake a course of self-study or participate in a supervised course of learning. It offers an invaluable distillation of government guidance and practice wisdom, a carefully paced modular approach to learning, and encouragement of ongoing critical reflection on continuing issues and dilemmas that need to be constantly addressed to ensure good practice.

The workbook contains:

- a learning profile at the start

- nine sessions

- a learning outcome profile at the end

- a review to assist reflection on what has been learned and applying it in practice

- a bibliography to help further learning

- an appendix listing key pieces of relevant legislation

- an appendix that sets out an action model to follow if abuse is suspected.

This manual gives **advice to anyone who is supervising their learning**, such as teachers or trainers, on using this package with their students or workers.

A section at the back of this manual explains how the methods used to supply and update the workbook materials:

- provide affordable training and learning solutions for all learners in both small and larger organisations

- allow you to preview here the training on a free trial. (If you do not want to use this manual and/or register for updates, please return this manual in clean and resalable condition for a full refund.)

- will keep you fully up-to-date with new material from the author.

- let students and practitioners undertake learning at their own pace and in their own time.

- give you reason to stay in contact with your learners, and them reason to want to stay in contact with you, so that you can add your own notes and supervision to their learning, and keep your own records of it.

We recommend that you make an early examination of the section starting on page 119 entitled *Updates, copying permission and electronic supply of The Safeguarding Vulnerable Adults Workbook*. This contains essential material on various options for use of the manual in teaching and training across your organisation.

As explained there, you can additionally purchase the workbook as a PDF. The PDF is adaptable for local use. So, for example, although the workbook has been developed principally for use in England, the PDF could be adapted for use in Scotland, Wales and Northern Ireland.

The following example is an actual update provided by the author on Friday 18th July 2008 relating to the Bournewood Judgement and the deprivation of liberty, discussed on pages 105-7.

This has been a very busy year in the world of Adult Protection. The Mental Capacity Act 2005 *(MCA 2005) is now in force and local authorities have now recruited IMCAs to help vulnerable people who lack capacity understand the nature and scope of decisions that need to be made.*

The Mental Health Act 2007 *(MHA 2007) has amended the* MCA 2005 *introducing new deprivation of liberty safeguards. Although the new need for authorisations doesn't come into effect until April, 2009 we need to begin to put the required mechanisms in place now. Local authorities need to appoint best interest assessors as part of the new six part assessment process to be followed before a vulnerable adult lacking capacity can be removed to a care home or long stay hospital or have their movements restricted. Schedule 9 of the* MHA 2007 *allows for certain exemptions – most amazingly – Section 47, of the* National Assistance Act 1948 *(NAA 1948) as the Department of Health has not had to respond to an EU ruling on this Section.*

Further regular up-dating will explore new measures in detail as they are defined more clearly, and each year you will be notified when a completely updated version of the workbook is available. To receive this updating service, register your purchase of this manual with the publisher, using the form on page 127.

About the author and consultant editor

Author

Denis Hart worked for over 16 years in residential childcare, eventually becoming the Head of the Regional Assessment Centre at Aycliffe, County Durham. He has taught at Bristol University, Nottingham Trent University and been a Principal Lecturer at the University of Teesside since 1991. Denis has been interested in protecting vulnerable adults since the roll-out of *No Secrets* and has been involved in developing and delivering an accredited training programme for people from a variety of professions. He has published widely on using the law in social work and is the co-editor of *Mental Health Nursing*.

Consultant editor

Robert Adams is Professor of Social Work at the University of Teesside. He has written and edited more than 80 books about social work and social policy, including several best-selling texts and the fourth edition of the international title *Empowerment and Participation in Social Work*, translated into Korean and Japanese.

Acknowledgements

The author and consultant editor would like to acknowledge the support of Wade Tovey, University of Teesside for the development of the training courses for practitioners in the Tees Valley which have contributed to the development of this package. Also, we should like to thank Geoffrey Mann of RHP for his patience and detailed work on the arrangements for supplying electronic copies.

Introduction

Using this Package

This package of materials can be used across your organisation in the training and teaching of anyone who has, or who will have contact with vulnerable adults. It can be used:

- With students in college or university

- With practitioners, such as carers and social workers, as part of their training at work

The workbook is a stand-alone resource for students and practitioners containing:

- a learning profile at the start

- nine sessions

- a learning outcome profile at the end

- a review to assist reflection on what has been learned and applying it in practice

- a bibliography to help further learning

- an appendix listing key pieces of relevant legislation

- an appendix that sets out an action model to follow if abuse is suspected

After the workbook is a section that describes in detail the photocopying permissions, electronic supply of materials and how to obtain regular updates (see p. ix for an example of an update).

The workbook offers an invaluable distillation of government guidance and practice wisdom, a carefully paced modular approach to learning, and encouragement of ongoing critical reflection on continuing issues and dilemmas that need to be constantly addressed to ensure good practice.

Many students should be able to use the entire workbook as a course of **self-study** which might take about 50 hours to complete.

But if needed, or if you prefer, you can add your own **supervision**, perhaps asking learners to discuss each section with you, and only distributing one section to them at a time. This way you can choose whether to let members of a group of learners progress at different speeds, or work their way through the workbook together, perhaps linking it to lectures, assignments or seminars. The trainer might present some material and some might involve the individuals working together on activities or in group discussion. Each session can be used as the basis for a half day training course and the nine sessions together can form the basis of a one week training course.

On first receiving this manual

When you first receive this manual, it is recommended that:

1. Don't worry about the publication date printed in this manual if it seems out of date. As described later in this introduction, this manual is just part of the training package, which the author aims to keep up-to-date, communicating with you via the publisher.

2. Look at the workbook to get a sense of the style of learning that is offered and the type of material that is covered. If this learning style and the type of material does not suit your needs, you may return this manual in clean and resalable condition for full credit.

3. But if it is going to meet your needs, **register now to receive licence to use it across you organisation and notification of updates**:

    (a) First read carefully the section on page 119 *Updates, copying permission and electronic supply of The* Safeguarding Vulnerable Adults *Workbook*.
    (b) Take particular care to familiarise yourself with the relevant terms and conditions; and guidance on expectations about responsible and respectful use of the copying rights and electronic materials. Note that different conditions apply to small and large organisations.
    (c) Then tear out and complete the form at the back of this manual and send it to the publisher at their address, as indicated on the form. (If there is no form at the back, then someone else must have already used it. If so, please phone 01297 443948 to purchase your own copy of this manual with a form for you to use.)

The content, scope and value of the workbook

The *Safeguarding Vulnerable Adults* package as a whole:

• lets students and workers undertake the learning at their own pace and in their own time.

• gives you reason to stay in contact with your learners, and them to want to stay in contact with you, so that you can add your own notes and supervision to their learning, and keep your own records of it.

This workbook is designed for everyone who has contact with vulnerable adults who may be abused. It begins with *No Secrets* and looks at the issues involved in devising local procedures and setting up multi-agency adult protection teams.

It looks at the key issues in identifying and progressing concerns about abuse in the home, in the community, in a day care facility or in a care home. Important background material is provided on Human Rights issues of working across professional boundaries and about domestic violence.

The key problem of capacity emerges as a theme throughout and the provisions of the *Mental Capacity Act 2005* are covered in depth. Also included are the *Safeguarding Vulnerable Groups Act 2006* and relevant aspects of the new *Mental Health Act 2007*. Subsequent legislation and guidance will be covered in the updates, as described earlier.

There is a learning profile at the beginning for learners to complete and an identical learning outcome profile at the end so they can monitor for themselves how useful the materials have been for developing knowledge and improving the basis upon which skills can be enhanced. But it is up to you, the supervisor of their learning, to use the material in the *Safeguarding Vulnerable Adults* workbook in ways that best fit into your overall teaching or training.

Working together to enable up-to-date teaching

The guidance set out in the section *Updates, copying permission and electronic supply of The Safeguarding Vulnerable Adults Workbook* is based on:

- respect for the author's copyright
- the view that their work in developing carefully distilled and critical learning materials to help you improve the training of people who work with vulnerable adults deserves to be remunerated.

The publisher and author therefore seek everyone's respectful and responsible and honourable co-operation in use of their work within the terms and conditions that have already been set out.

What the complete package offers

Reciprocating this respect and responsible co-operation, the publisher and author have:

- Put in place the processes described at the end of this manual that enable organisations to copy and digitally copy the workbook, with a minimum of fuss, for use by their learners.
- Kept the costs of obtaining these permissions at sensibly low levels by using appropriate, rather than the most sophisticated, technologies.
- Included, within this, suitable arrangements for both large and smaller organisations.
- Kept the introductory price of buying this initial manual well within the budgets of large and smaller organisations. Everyone with responsibility for safeguarding vulnerable adults can assess the value to them of the author's work on a free trial basis. (If you do not want to use the *Safeguarding Vulnerable Adults* package, you can return this manual in clean and resaleable condition for full credit.)

Thank you. We hope that you will find this package useful and that it helps enhance practice with vulnerable adults.

For a complete schedule of updates as they are written to address changes in law and guidance, please visit www.russellhouse.co.uk and search for 'Safeguarding Vulnerable Adults' where update information is prominently displayed. To obtain these updates, you will need to register your purchase of this manual by completing and submitting the form on pages 127 and 128.

The
Safeguarding Vulnerable Adults
Workbook

This stand-alone workbook is part of Denis A. Hart's
Safeguarding Vulnerable Adults: A Training Package to Enhance Practice
(Russell House Publishing).

SAFEGUARDING VULNERABLE ADULTS

A Workbook for Enhancing Practice for Students and Practitioners

Denis A. Hart

Consultant editor Robert Adams

Russell House Publishing

Important Notices!

1. Please ensure that you are reading the most up-to-date version of this workbook.

Look at the © year at the foot of each page of this workbook. If you are reading this notice later than April in the following calendar year, please check with your supervisor that they have given you the most up-to-date version of the workbook. The publisher and author aim to notify them each year – usually in April/May – about buying an updated version of the workbook for use in the new local authority and academic years.

If you have questions you may contact the publisher.
Russsell House Publishing Limited
4 St George's House
Uplyme Road Business Park
Lyme Regis
Dorset DT7 3LS
email: help@russellhouse.co.uk   www.russellhouse.co.uk

This material has been copied and/or adapted from their publication:

Safeguarding Vulnerable Adults: a training package to enhance practice.
© Denis Hart 2008   ISBN 978-1-905541-37-9

For any other information about the copyright, the publisher, the author and his moral rights to this work, which we ask you to respect, please see that original work.

2. Please use this workbook respectfully and responsibly

This workbook has been copied to you, either digitally or on paper by a university or employer at which establishment you are undertaking learning or training. Your university and employer will have done this with permission of the copyright holder and publisher.

If it has been copied to you under any other circumstances, it will very probably be a breach of copyright for you to be in possession of this copy, and you should seek specific reassurance from whoever gave it to you that you and they are not breaking the law.

Under no circumstances should you copy this material to anyone else. If anyone else asks you for a copy, please advise them to ask for one from their university or employer. Only by obtaining their copy in this way can they be sure to receive, through their supervisor or lecturer (who will be receiving periodic updates from the publisher) the full and necessary support of their learning, which may otherwise be out-of-date as government guidance changes.

3. Finally, please read carefully the section *Advice for learners using The Safeguarding Vulnerable Adults Workbook* before you start using the workbook.

Thank you for using this workbook in your studies and employment. We hope that it helps in your studies and in your work with vulnerable adults.

Geoffrey Mann, Managing Director, Russell House Publishing Ltd.

The *Safeguarding Vulnerable Adults* **Workbook**

Contents

Safeguarding Vulnerable Adults. © 2008 Denis A. Hart. www.russellhouse.co.uk

Why we must all work to safeguard vulnerable adults

Robert Adams, Professor of Social Work, University of Teesside

This authoritative package prepared by Denis Hart is a welcome and timely addition to the resources available to tackle and prevent abuse to adults.

There is growing acknowledgement of the longstanding problem of abuse and maltreatment of adults, both in Britain and other Western countries. However, it is scandalous that despite intermittent glimpses of this in Britain over past decades and despite the repeated shining of the spotlight of inquiries and investigations into the abuse of children, governments and research institutions have not been moved until the twenty first century to establish a professional baseline for understanding and tackling the safeguarding of adults. It is an ironic sign of the times, perhaps, that Comic Relief provided part of the funding for the survey, which attempted to provide nationally representative estimates of the abuse of older people, both in public and private care and at home (O'Keeffe et al., 2007). The results of this survey are pretty shocking. An estimated 227,000 people aged 66 and over – 2.6 per cent or 1 in 40 of the total population – have experienced abuse or maltreatment over the year 2006-7, either by a relative, friend or care worker. If we widen the net to include maltreatment involving neighbours and acquaintances the total increases by about a half, to 4 per cent, or 342,000 older people subjected to some form of abuse. Bearing in mind that the respondents to the survey were able to identify more than one abusing person, over half of the abusers (51 per cent) were spouses, 49 per cent another member of the family, 13 per cent a care worker and 5 per cent a close friend. The most common form of abuse was neglect, then financial abuse, then physical and psychological abuse and finally sexual abuse.

Whereas older people in the above-quoted survey, perhaps surprisingly, identify neglect and financial abuse as more prevalent than other forms of abuse, disabled people experience slightly different, but no less serious, forms of abuse. A survey of blind people (Action for Blind People, 2008) for instance, estimated that 60 per cent of the approximately 2m visually impaired people in the UK have experienced physical or verbal abuse.

The particular contribution of this package by Denis Hart is the detailed, step-by-step attention it gives to each aspect of safeguarding. It is authoritatively written and the legislation and procedures on which it is based have been meticulously researched in order to make it as up to date as possible. It provides the basis on which to develop better professional practice.

I commend the package to you.

Robert Adams

References

Action for Blind People (2008) *Report on Verbal and Physical Abuse towards Blind and Partially Sighted People across the UK.* London: Action for Blind People.

O'Keeffe et al. (2007) *UK National Study of Abuse and Neglect of Older People: (Prevalence Survey Report)* London: NatCen.

Advice for learners using The *Safeguarding Vulnerable Adults* Workbook

This workbook offers:

- an invaluable distillation of government guidance and practice wisdom

- a carefully paced modular approach to learning

- encouragement of ongoing critical reflection on continuing issues and dilemmas that need to be constantly addressed to ensure good practice in your current and future work.

It can be used:

- in the training and teaching of anyone who has, or who will have contact with vulnerable adults

- by students in college or university

- by practitioners, such as carers and social workers, as part of their training at work

It can be used as a course of self-study, but our recommendation is that **your learning from this workbook should be supervised by your lecturer at university, or by your supervisor at work**.

- They can register with the publisher to receive news on changes in government guidance and practice wisdom, and incorporate such changes into your learning.

- They can add their experience and knowledge to what is in this workbook to assist your ongoing critical reflection on how you can best safeguard the vulnerable adults in your care.

If we are able to organise a sensible way of directly supporting learners and practitioners through their careers, in addition to the current focus on supporting their supervisors and lecturers, we will post notices about this on our website at www.russellhouse.co.uk. But until then, it needs to be clearly stated that this workbook is not a substitute for teaching at university or supervision at work.

The workbook contains:

- a learning profile at the start

- 9 sessions

- a learning outcome profile at the end

- a review to assist reflection on what has been learned and applying it in practice

- a bibliography to help further learning
- an appendix listing key pieces of relevant legislation
- an appendix that sets out an action model to follow if abuse is suspected.

The content, scope and value of the workbook

This workbook is designed for everyone who has contact with vulnerable adults who may be abused. It begins with *No Secrets* and looks at the issues involved in devising local procedures and setting up multi-agency adult protection teams.

It looks at the key issues in identifying and progressing concerns about abuse in the home, in the community, in a day care facility or in a care home. Important background material is provided on Human Rights issues of working across professional boundaries and about domestic violence.

The key problem of capacity emerges as a theme throughout and the provisions of the *Mental Capacity Act 2005* are covered in depth. Also included are the *Safeguarding Vulnerable Groups Act 2006* and relevant aspects of the new *Mental Health Act 2007*. Subsequent legislation and guidance will be covered in the updates, as described earlier.

There is a learning profile at the beginning for learners to complete and an identical learning outcome checklist at the end so you can monitor for yourself:

- How useful the materials have been for developing knowledge and improving the basis upon which your skills can be enhanced.

- How what you have learned in The *Safeguarding Vulnerable Adults* Workbook can be incorporated into your wider learning and practice.

- How it can help ensure that you play your part in the crucial work of safeguarding all vulnerable adults with whom you may have contact.

About the author and consultant editor

Author

Denis Hart worked for over 16 years in residential childcare, eventually becoming the Head of the Regional Assessment Centre at Aycliffe, County Durham. He has taught at Bristol University, Nottingham Trent University and been a Principal Lecturer at the University of Teesside since 1991. Denis has been interested in protecting vulnerable adults since the roll-out of *No Secrets* and has been involved in developing and delivering an accredited training programme for people from a variety of professions. He has published widely on using the law in social work and is the co-editor of *Mental Health Nursing*.

Consultant editor

Robert Adams is Professor of Social Work at the University of Teesside. He has written and edited more than 80 books about social work and social policy, including several best-selling texts and the fourth edition of the international title *Empowerment and Participation in Social Work*, translated into Korean and Japanese.

Acknowledgements

The author and consultant editor would like to acknowledge the support of Wade Tovey, University of Teesside for the development of the training courses for practitioners in the Tees Valley which have contributed to the development of this package. Also, we should like to thank Geoffrey Mann of RHP for his patience and detailed work on the arrangements for supplying electronic copies.

Learning Profile

Below is a list of learning objectives for this workbook. You can use it to help you to identify the extent to which you are already familiar with the material covered in this book.

For each of the statments listed below, tick the box that most closely corresponds to your starting point. This will give you a profile of your learning needs in the areas covered in each session of this workbook.

The profile is repeated at the end of the book as 'Learning Outcomes': and you can check your progress by going through it again then.

Session One

I can:

	Not at all	*Partly*	*Very well*
• Explain the origin of *No Secrets*.	☐	☐	☐
• Summarise its main objectives.	☐	☐	☐

Session Two

I can:

	Not at all	*Partly*	*Very well*
• Identify informal and formal aspects of inter-agency co-operation.	☐	☐	☐
• Explain how multi-agency teams were created, and their main purposes.	☐	☐	☐
• Explain what is meant by 'lead body' and its implications for practice.	☐	☐	☐

Session Three

I can:

	Not at all	*Partly*	*Very well*
• Identify the key stakeholders in *No Secrets*.	☐	☐	☐
• Explain the need to establish a multi-agency management committee (adult protection).	☐	☐	☐
• Explain why *No Secrets* has not been underpinned by new legislation.	☐	☐	☐

Session Four

I can:

	Not at all	Partly	Very well
Identify where abuse is likely to take place.	☐	☐	☐
Describe the procedures already in place for investigating certain types of abuse and complaints.	☐	☐	☐
Pin-point gaps in current provisions to protect vulnerable adults.	☐	☐	☐

Session Five

I can:

	Not at all	Partly	Very well
Have awareness of the challenges presented by the implementation of *No Secrets*.	☐	☐	☐
Identify things I can contribute.	☐	☐	☐
Confirm my understanding of the various kinds of abuse which can occur.	☐	☐	☐
Explain the role of the multi-agency management committee and the vulnerable adults protection team.	☐	☐	☐
Outline why investigation procedures are necessary.	☐	☐	☐

Session Six

I can:

	Not at all	Partly	Very well
Outline the key principles underpinning effective practice.	☐	☐	☐
Detail the key issues in assessing risk.	☐	☐	☐
Describe the range of outcomes that can follow from an initial concern.	☐	☐	☐

Session Seven

I can:

	Not at all	Partly	Very well
• Describe the dilemmas that confront *professionals* responding to domestic violence.	☐	☐	☐
• Explain how the nature of privacy may affect my response to domestic violence.	☐	☐	☐
• Describe legal provisions to protect victims of domestic violence and which enable them to remain in their own homes.	☐	☐	☐

Session Eight

I can:

	Not at all	Partly	Very well
• Outline the principles which apply when determining capacity and describe the practical test used to determine capacity.	☐	☐	☐
• Explain the **new** provisions contained in the *Mental Capacity Act 2005*.	☐	☐	☐
• Describe the dilemmas posed by capacity and compulsion.	☐	☐	☐

Session Nine

I can:

	Not at all	Partly	Very well
• Describe the main provisions of the *Mental Capacity Act 2005*.	☐	☐	☐
• Explain how finances are protected.	☐	☐	☐
• Explain how healthcare and treatment issues are dealt with for people who lack capacity.	☐	☐	☐
• Describe what is meant by an advance decision and explain how, and when, these should be used.	☐	☐	☐

Session One: What is *No Secrets*?

Session objectives

Upon completing this session you should be able to:

- Explain the origin of *No Secrets*.

- Summarise its main objectives.

Introduction

No Secrets is:
'Guidance on developing and implementing multi-agency policies and procedures to protect vulnerable adults from abuse', produced jointly by:

- The Department of Health

and

- The Home Office.

The Guidance arose from:

1. Several incidents which demonstrated the need for:

    . . . immediate action to ensure that vulnerable adults, who are at risk of abuse, receive protection and support.

    (*No Secrets*, 2000: 6)

2. The Human Rights Act 1998 and the government's:

    . . . firm intention to close a significant gap in the delivery of those rights.

    (op cit: 6)

In a nutshell, *No Secrets* strives to protect vulnerable adults from abuse.

The following activity is designed to help you think about this further.

Activity 1.1

This activity should take you about 5 minutes to complete.

Write down three or four ways in which you believe vulnerable adults could be abused.

Comment

To prevent abuse we need to understand the various forms it can take. You probably began by thinking about physical abuse as this is probably the *most visible* and then went on to think of other aspects such as:

- sexual abuse
- psychological abuse
- financial exploitation

No Secrets recognises these, but *also adds:*

- neglect and acts of omission (failure to provide appropriate care)
- discriminatory abuse

defining abuse as:

> . . . *a violation of an individual's human and civil rights by any other person or persons.*

(op cit: 9)

Abuse in any form:

> . . . *may consist of a single act or repeated acts.*

Who are vulnerable adults?

Having looked at the range of possible activities which may constitute abuse we now need to think about which adults are vulnerable.

The Guidance applies to 'all vulnerable adults *over 18*' and for our present purpose we can assume this refers to the same groups of people defined as vulnerable under *The Police and Criminal Evidence Act 1984* notably:

- older people with conditions such as Alzheimer's or dementia
- people with learning disabilities
- people with mental illness.

Indeed, all these groups of service users are included, with one important addition:

- people with other forms of disability.

The definition used in *No Secrets* was taken from *Who Decides?* published by the Lord Chancellors Department in 1997, and includes *any* person:

. . . who is or may be in need of community care services by reason of mental or other disability, age or illness and who is unable to take care of him or herself or unable to protect him or herself against significant harm or exploitation.

A new definition has been provided under Section 59 of the *Safeguarding Vulnerable Groups Act 2006*, as you will learn later on, but at present the new definition is *only* to be used when working under the *Safeguarding Vulnerable Groups Act 2006*.

The following activity is designed to refresh your memory as to the way the law determines *how* disability is defined and *how* the need for community care services is determined.

Activity 1.2

This activity should take you about 15 minutes to complete.

1. See if you can remember the definition of people with disability under Section 29 of the *National Assistance Act 1948* and write it down in your own words. (Don't worry if you can't remember it exactly as we will reproduce it below.)

2. Make a note of the Section of the *NHS and Community Care Act (NHSCCA) 1990* which allows for the assessment of people with needs, and what you think it allows you to do.

Comment

1. The definition used in Section 29, *National Assistance Act 1948* is:

   . . . persons aged 18 or over who are blind, deaf or dumb or suffer from mental disorder of any kind and other persons aged 18 or over who are substantially or permanently handicapped by illness, injury or congenital deformity or such other disability as may be prescribed.

'Development' means physical, intellectual, emotional, social or behavioural development.

'Health' means physical or mental health.

Older people are not included in the definition but are included as being eligible for Community Care Services.

2. The section of the *NHSCCA, 1990* which deals with assessment of need is Section 47(1). There is a duty on the local authority to conduct an assessment if it appears that the person is in need of a community care service.

Furthermore, if it appears that they are disabled, the local authority must conduct a *further* assessment under Section 47(2) to:

- consider their entitlement to services under the *Disabled Persons (Services, Consultation and Representation) Act 1986* as specified in Section 2 of the *Chronically Sick and Disabled Persons Act 1970*.

The structure of *No Secrets*

We have so far looked at why such Guidance became necessary and at the people to whom it should apply. We now present you with an overview of the rest of the Guidance.

Section 3 required local authorities to 'Set up an inter-agency framework'. Those people who have experience of working with children and families will make obvious connections to *Working Together under the Children Act 1989* (DoH, 1990) and the establishment of Area Child Protection Committees (ACPCs) now know as Safeguarding Boards.

Section 4 deals with 'Developing inter-agency policy' and looks at what can be identified as 'common ground' between the agencies so that the risk of conflict is minimised.

Section 5 moves on to look at the 'Main elements of strategy' including issues such as:

- Training staff and volunteers to act appropriately and consistently.
- Commissioning of services and contract monitoring.
- Concerns about confidentiality which arise whenever agencies *share* information about vulnerable people.

Section 6 is about putting the strategy into effective practice. Entitled 'Procedures for responding in individual cases', it looks at the key areas to be covered when:

- Investigating suspected abuse.
- Carrying out assessments.
- Recording interventions.

and also

- Outlines some of the possible actions which can be taken.

Finally, Section 7 is 'Getting the message across'; essentially how do we heighten awareness about the issue of abuse of vulnerable adults.

Although *No Secrets* is an important initiative and no one can question its importance in *protecting* vulnerable adults, it nevertheless is set in a *very different legal context* to child protection work.

As this workbook is not only designed to help you learn, but also develop your thinking, we end this session with a Review Activity to get you to look at the potential challenges of *No Secrets*.

Review Activity

This activity should take you about 15 minutes to complete.

Dorothy Parkes is an 81-year-old with partial mobility who lives with her son. The GP has telephoned to say he is concerned about bruising he's seen on Dorothy which he doesn't believe can be attributed to an accident.

Think about the *issues* and write down two or three of them.

Comment

The issues you may have considered are:

1. Do I have a *legal* duty to investigate the GP's claims?

2. How should I approach Dorothy who might be able to take action in her own right?

    Although Dorothy is 81 years of age it is important to treat her with respect and to empower her to pursue actions in her own right even if you are going to provide her with some support.

3. Does Dorothy have capacity?

4. What rights does her son have under the *Human Rights Act 1998*? Do the son's rights extend to being allowed to abuse or harm another person living in that home?

It is interesting to note here that if the GP had referred a child to you with the same concerns you would have:

- A legal mandate to investigate under Section 47 of the *Children Act 1989*.

- A clear understanding of your duties, powers and responsibilities through the policy guidance issued by the local Area Child Protection Committee.

and

- A right to make enquiries in the home without offending the *Human Rights Act 1998*.

The issues you have considered raise the need to create similar policies and structures when working with other vulnerable people so that practitioners are not left to struggle in isolation. *No Secrets* helps us by focusing our minds on the issues.

The fourth issue we have identified reflects the importance of keeping up to date with the legal context of practice. Only two or three years ago practitioners would have been reluctant to intervene as they would have been apprehensive of breaching the *Human Rights Act 1998* notably the Right to Respect of Privacy in family life. However, as a result of case law (decisions made by courts when *interpreting* the law) it is now generally accepted that one person's right to privacy does not entitle them to use that right in the home to abuse another person living in the household.

As safeguarding is inevitably delivered in a multi-agency context, it is this aspect we will now explore in the next session.

Session Two: Inter-disciplinary Approaches to Good Practice

Session objectives

Upon completing this session you should be able to:

- Identify informal and formal aspects of inter-agency co-operation.

- Explain how multi-agency teams were created, and their main purposes.

- Explain what is meant by 'lead body' and its implications for practice.

Introduction

No Secrets requires agencies involved in social care to work together in a much more consistent and co-ordinated way.

Taylor (1997) argued that partnership requires agencies to change their cultures:

> *Effective partnership is not easy. It requires allocation of responsibility within partner organisations, with resources, time and incentive structures for partnership working. Partners need to be prepared to change their cultures and ways of operating to accommodate voluntary sector, community and user participants.*
>
> (Taylor, 1997)

To achieve this we need to re-orientate traditional thinking so as to focus upon:

> *delivering an effective and appropriate response to service users*

rather than concerning ourselves with developing inward looking policies and strategies essentially about the self defence of the agency.

An agency's culture can be seen as a system. The degree to which it is open or closed depends upon:

- Any legal duties placed on it to work collaboratively.

and

- Its attitude towards collaboration.

Payne (2000) identified three systems, or networks, which he believed help people:

- **Informal or natural systems**, such as family, friends or fellow workers.

- **Formal systems** such as community groups or trade unions.

- **Social systems** such as hospitals or schools.

Pincus and Minahan (1973) identified three potential relationships social workers or social carers can develop with others:

- **Collaborative** – whenever there is a shared purpose.

- **Bargaining** – where an agreement needs to be reached.

- **Conflict** – whenever purposes are in opposition.

Activity 2.1

This activity should take you about 5 minutes to complete.

From what you have learnt so far about *No Secrets* write down two or three aspects that might lead to collaboration, bargaining or conflict between agencies.

Comment

Your response is likely to be determined by the agency you work for and your role within it. However, we have tried to pull out some common themes.

- **Collaborative** – *No Secrets* is about collaboration and the establishment of commonly understood and shared policies and procedures.

- **Bargaining** – The multi-agency forum is a place where differing ideologies meet. *Health* may adopt the view that confidentiality is absolute, whereas *social care* may believe that, like child abuse, the abuse of a vulnerable adult must be properly addressed even if this entails *sharing* confidential information with other professional bodies.

- **Conflict** – An advocacy group or service user group may want all cases of *established* abuse treated as criminal matters, but representatives of carers may feel that this would result in many carers dropping out as they may not want the additional stress of being investigated, even of being charged by the police.

This has become even more pertinent with the advent of new criminal charges introduced by Section 44 of the *Mental Capacity Act 2005* from October, 2007 notably:

- The ill treatment, or willful neglect of a vulnerable adult.

Approaches to inter-agency co-operation

Essentially there are four kinds of working together:

- informal networking
- formal networking
- inter-agency collaboration
- multi-agency working

As workers in the social care arena, we are likely to get involved with colleagues from other agencies as part of day-to-day good practice. Put simply, as we get to know people who work in other professions, we start to trust them and respect their views and thereby become able to consult with each other informally as and when individual issues arise.

Hart (1998) explains:

Informal networking often begins when a worker needs to access a service or a resource provided by a worker in another agency. As we get to know the person better we may discover that we also:

- *share a common concern or interest*
- *have similar expertise*
- *are able to exchange ideas*
- *trust and respect each other*

As a result we become more accessible to each other.

(Hart, 1998: 33)

However, there can be downsides to this approach as well.

Activity 2.2

This activity should take you about 15 minutes to complete.

What in your own experience have you found to be the advantages and challenges in developing informal networks both with other agencies and service users?

Draw up two columns, one for advantages and one for potential challenges, and itemise three or four aspects of each.

Comment

Here is our list. It is not definitive and you may have noted a number of other aspects as well.

Advantages

Using informal networks workers can short circuit procedures when these are considered to be cumbersome or overly bureaucratic.

Can provide social workers and social care workers with enhanced professional understanding of the task.

Offers service users a support group.

Can potentially offer service users a wider range of provision and resources. Indeed the *Community Care (Carers Recognition) Act 1995* formally recognises such an approach.

Builds upon service users' own strengths and preferences rather than imposing professional will or authority.

Potential challenges

May infringe equal opportunities by giving a preferential service to those service users whose worker has established a strong informal network.

Can lead to some agencies becoming concerned that workers are spending too much time on what are considered to be distractions from the main job.

Informal networks may be exploited due to under-funding of essential support services from statutory bodies.

Could lead to informal provision taking over from what was previously provided formally.

If you are employed by a statutory body a conflict of interest may arise.

Formal networking

We'll introduce this approach by quoting from Henderson (1995):

> *Other statutory agencies are agencies which, like social work/social services have a legal function, duties and responsibilities. These include the local health authorities, local housing and local education departments. They affect the social work process because, in the early stages of referral and information gathering, it may become clear that another agency could provide information, or a better, more appropriate service to a service user other than social work/social services.*
>
> *. . . Another way to look at this is to visualise a dynamic approach in which a number of agencies co-operate.*
>
> (Henderson, 1995: 23)

If you work in the voluntary sector you are likely to have routine contact with a number of statutory agencies. If you work in social services you may have regular contact with a number of support groups, self-help groups and advocacy groups. The weakest link at the networking level, ironically, is often when statutory agencies make contact with other formal service providers.

Inter-agency collaboration

We have seen that networking is characterised by individual workers choosing to form links with other informal or formal groups, or by an individual agency establishing a range of informal contacts with others to develop a better co-ordinated service.

By contrast, inter-agency collaboration is created at a formal organisational level when two or more agencies agree to work together to share information or to jointly plan services.

Challis et al. (1994) argue that collaboration is necessary because of 'gaps in coverage, conflicts of aim and failures of communication'. They identify a number of forms collaboration could take, the most important being what they term 'rational planning', the aim of which is to produce 'a seamless service'. Rational planning has two stages, the second of which occurs only infrequently.

Stage 1

Agencies meet to identify available services and outline a formal network showing which agencies are providing which services.

Stage 2

Participating agencies develop a joint strategy for delivering and monitoring services and a procedure for reciprocal exchange.

Inter-agency collaboration has so far worked best when meeting the needs of individual service users. In this situation, agencies meet together formally to address a common problem or need. The meeting works particularly well if focused on case discussions or reviews. These:

- Enable differing perspectives to be shared constructively to respond to a common concern.
- Value each agency's unique contribution.
- Focus on the service user.
- Produce an agreed action plan stating who is going to do what, when and for what purpose.

Lead body responsibility

The law on inter-agency collaboration is quite clear and is set out in *No Secrets*.

Agencies may be required to:

- share information

or

- work together,

but

- in such a way that it does not contradict any agency's individual statutory responsibility or duty.

Until quite recently it was assumed that a particular range of services was always the responsibility of one specific public sector agency. Health services would seek to cure people who became sick, the education department would provide schools to ensure that children and young people receive the most appropriate education, and social services would act as a safety net to provide services to people who were vulnerable by virtue of lack of care, old age, disability or abuse.

Inter-agency collaboration and multi-agency or multi-disciplinary teams make these boundaries less clear cut. Whenever a number of agencies are required to work collaboratively, or choose to do so, the question arises of which agency will take an overall responsibility for the service being provided, and its quality. As a response to this issue there has developed the concept of a lead body.

(Hart, 1998: op cit: 43)

Ranson and Stewart (1994) remind us that:

Management in the public domain is . . . a process, subject to challenge and debate. The pressure is for greater rather than less accountability. There are demands for open government and in local authorities much wider access to information has been conceded. The model of management in the public domain has to accept and meet the requirements of public accountability.

(Ranson and Stewart, 1994: 57)

The idea of lead body enables an adequate response to be made to this drive for accountability, without compromising the principle of collaborative working.

Activity 2.3

This activity should take you about 10 minutes to complete. In the following scenario write down who you believe has lead responsibility?

Investigating an incident in a private care home where a number of residents were scalded by the bath water.

Comment

On the surface this should have been a very simple activity. *The Care Standards Act 2000* created the National Care Standards Commission, later the Care Standards Commission Inspectorate (CSCI) and to become the Care Quality Commission (CQC) to:

- register

- regulate

- inspect

all residential care facilities and all community care facilities with the exception of those run by lone traders. Therefore, ostensibly, the incident should be investigated by CSCI as potentially it could be:

- A regulatory problem, as the incident may well influence the decision to continue the home's registration.

In reality, CSCI tends to reject requests to investigate such incidents, preferring to pass such matters back to the local authority's Adult Protection Team to deal with, even though CSCI has specific powers to investigate, including:

- The removal of all written and computer-based records held on the premises.

- Interviewing all staff under Codes B and C of *PACE, 1984* even without consent.

- Interviewing, with consent, all residents under the Code.

Remember here that the local authority has no such powers!

Hence, we hope you have learnt here that:

- Identifying the lead agency is not always as easy in practice as it first appears.

Applying the best principles of collaboration in implementing *No Secrets*

Biggs (1997) argued that:

> *Inter-professional collaboration is often spoken of as a 'good thing' by policy makers, without examining possible differences in interpretation in greater detail. In reality it can refer to a variety of practices and relationships that form a sort of hinterland of meaning behind policy objectives. If these differences are not clarified, misunderstandings can multiply. Implicit assumptions held by participants then come into sharp relief as policy statements have to be translated into operations.*

(Biggs, in Ovretveit: 186)

To make *No Secrets* work effectively, the multi-agency management committee has to consult as wide a range of people as possible to get the fullest possible picture of abuse including issues such as:

- Who is vulnerable.

- What forms abuse can take.

- Where abuse can occur.

- What range of actions can be taken once abuse is established.

From the information gathered, the committees were able to:

- agree a set of 5 to 10 major categories of issues to be debated to *establish common ground*.

It was from this newly emergent, and expressed, common understanding that policies and procedures were developed and investigation arrangements put in place with a clear agenda. Nonetheless the problem remains that, unlike child protection where Section 47 of the *Children Act 1989* gives local authority a clear legal *DUTY* to investigate all cases of suspected child abuse, there is no such duty to investigate cases involving suspected abuse of vulnerable adults unless:

- That person wishes it.

- They lack capacity.

- An actual crime has been committed.

Review Activity

This activity should take you about 15 minutes to complete.

Imagine you are working as a professional carer with vulnerable adults and have been asked if you would like to become part of a new joint investigation team.

Write down three or four things you would want to check before expressing an interest.

Comment

You probably thought about issues such as:

1. Will my new role of investigator conflict with my motivation to care and support vulnerable people?

2. Will I receive specific training in this area as it is new to me?

3. Will the team be multi-disciplinary and how do I feel about working with other bodies?

4. How stressful is this going to be?

To address these:

1. Protecting vulnerable adults should be carried out in a sensitive way respecting the individual person's rights and wishes and so *should not* be in conflict with your desire to care and support but rather add to it.

2. You should receive training on *No Secrets* if you work with vulnerable adults *regardless* of any request to you to join an investigation team.

3. Child Protection Teams and Youth Offending Teams provide excellent examples of people from different backgrounds coming together and devising more consistent, effective and creative strategies for intervention with individuals.

4. It will only be stressful if we do not have clear policies and procedures and an awareness as to who to consult and when.

In this session we have looked at *how* we can work together effectively. We now move on to look at *whom* we need to engage in the process of better protection for vulnerable people, i.e. who are the stakeholders.

Session Three: Stakeholders in *No Secrets*

Session objectives

Upon completing this session you should be able to:

- Identify the key stakeholders in *No Secrets.*

- Explain the need to establish a multi-agency management committee (adult protection).

- Explain why *No Secrets* has not been underpinned by new legislation.

Introduction

In the last session we looked at the types of approaches which can be adopted in multi-agency working. In this session we will focus on the various agencies who need to come together to effectively protect vulnerable adults. Not surprisingly, the stakeholders in *No Secrets* are, in the main, those groups who have an established interest in community care.

The following activity is designed to help you check your understanding.

Activity 3.1

This activity should take you about 5 minutes to complete.

Write down whom you believe are the stakeholders in community care.

As *No Secrets* is about protecting vulnerable adults from abuse, see if you can think of some other agencies or groups of people who will need to be included.

Comment

You probably began by thinking about:

- service users

- their carers

- social care

- the police

- health

and

- other service providers such as the voluntary and private sectors.

In many ways, you are creating a similar body to that already established to handle cases of child protection, i.e. the Safeguarding Board (formerly known as Area Child Protection Committee), but *No Secrets* goes beyond this and has required that an inter-agency administrative framework is established to include:

- commissioners of health and social care services

- providers of health and social care services

- providers of sheltered and supported housing

- regulators of services

- the police and other relevant law enforcement agencies (including the Crown Prosecution Service)

- voluntary and private agencies

- other local authority departments, e.g. housing and education

- probation departments

- DSS Benefits Agencies

- carer support groups

- user groups and user-led services

- advocacy and advisory services

- community safety partnerships

- services meeting the needs of specific groups experiencing violence

- agencies offering legal advice and representation.

(op cit: 14–15)

Working together

When 'Working Together' with children and families you are working to a legal mandate as laid down by the *Children Act 1989*.

There is a general duty to investigate allegations of child abuse (physical, sexual, emotional or discriminatory) under Section 47(1) and also a general duty to:

safeguard and promote the welfare of children' under Section 17.

This means local authorities must:

- Promote the upbringing of children by their families.

- Provide a range of services in the area that will help families to look after their children.

The way in which local authorities are expected to achieve this is set down in Schedule 2 of the Act.

The current Government Guidance on working with children and families is to be found in *Quality Protects*, which lays down eight National Objectives. However, these objectives do not pose problems for local authorities as they are almost identical to those concerns listed in the *welfare checklist* which courts use in child protection cases as a direct result of Section 1(3) of the *Children Act 1989*.

Activity 3.2

This activity should take you about 15 minutes to complete.

We have just seen how *Working Together* with children and families is made effective in practice by being underpinned by law.

Now turn your thinking to *Working Together to Protect Vulnerable Adults from Abuse*.

What is your understanding of the law here and what specific problems could arise in multi-agency working?

Comment

Initially, there was a major problem about *Working Together* with vulnerable adults because there was no parallel legislation to underpin it.

Practitioners have found themselves in the same paradoxical position as child protection workers prior to the *Children Act 1989*, i.e. damned for doing and damned for not doing.

On one hand, some practitioners wished to follow traditional values and *empower* a vulnerable adult to make their own choice. (This could mean they chose not to report an assault on themselves or chose to remain at home rather than be re-housed or placed in some form of residential care.)

On the other hand, others felt uncomfortable that a vulnerable adult could chose to stay at home with a person who they believe is abusing them or financially exploiting them.

Article 8 of the European Convention lays down the:

> *Right to respect for family and private life.*

So the question arises: 'Can I intrude and under what circumstances?'

No Secrets recognises this quandary. Paragraph 2.19 states:

> *The seriousness or extent of abuse is often not clear when anxiety is first expressed. It is important, therefore, when considering the appropriateness of intervention, to approach reports of incidents or allegations with an open mind.*

(op cit: 12–13)

A number of factors are suggested for consideration:

- *the **vulnerability** of the individual*
- *the **nature and extent** of the abuse*
- *the **length of time** it has been occurring*
- *the **impact** on the individual*

and

- *the risk of **repeated and increasingly serious** acts involving this or other vulnerable adults.*

Remember also here how case law is developing to prohibit one person from using their Right to privacy from abusing another living in the household.

The need for establishing new structures

No Secrets required local authorities to set up:

- a multi-agency management committee (adult protection)

and

- a joint investigation team.

The functions of the management committee are to:

- Identify agreed objectives and priorities for its work.
- Determine policy.
- Co-ordinate activity between agencies.
- Facilitate joint training.
- Monitor and review progress.

The functions of the joint investigation team are almost identical to that of the child protection team, notably to:

- Operate to agreed common procedures.

- Investigate complaints.

- Consider any action appropriate with regard to criminal proceedings.

- Consider any implications relating to regulation, inspection and contract monitoring.

- Consider action to be taken by employers such as supervision, disciplinary proceedings, use of complaints or grievance procedures and any action necessary to remove the perpetrator from the professional register or refer them to the Independent Safeguarding Authority.

However, because of the legal quandary posed by the *Human Rights Act 1998*, to ensure proper treatment of both:

- victim

and

- alleged abuser (where appropriate).

the teams need to consider any:

- Assessment and care planning issues which may arise for the vulnerable person who has been abused.

- Arrangements for the treatment or care of the abuser where, say, for example, they are the primary carer.

There are enormous benefits from this:

> *A properly co-ordinated joint investigation will achieve more than a series of separate investigations. It will ensure that evidence is shared, repeated interviewing is avoided and will cause less distress for the person who may have suffered abuse. Good co-ordination will also take into account the different methods of gathering and presenting evidence and the different requirements with regard to standard of proof. The communication needs of victims including people with sensory impairments, learning disabilities, dementia or whose first language is not English must be taken into account. Interviewers and interpreters may need specific training.*

(op cit: 29)

The following activity has been designed to help you think about this further.

Activity 3.3

This activity should take about 15 minutes to complete.

In making a home visit to Arthur, a 72-year-old retired police sergeant who lives with his 42-year-old son, you become concerned about bruising about the body. You don't believe these were from a fall, or some other accident.

For now assume that local Inter-agency Policy, Procedures and Practice Guidance *do not* exist.

1. List any legal issues which may need to be considered.

2. Think carefully about what you might do and why. Write down what you have decided.

Comment

1. Whereas in cases of child protection you have clear legal duties and a procedure for action, there are no equivalent duties and procedures when it comes to older people, other than to make a referral to Safeguarding (Adult Protection).

2. In deciding what to do you may have considered reporting the matter to the police, but you will need to be careful that the service user wishes to pursue such a course of action, or they lack capacity and you have good grounds for believing Arthur's injuries were non-accidental and inflicted by his son.

Prior to the production of local Policy and Guidance, you would have most likely decided to discuss the visit with your line manager in the first instance to test out how serious your concerns were and to address the issues posed.

You may have considered:

*   What the service user wants, bearing in mind that he will be feeling isolated and fearful, with possible anxieties about going into residential care and fear of retaliation from the abuser.

*   Implications arising from the *Human Rights Act 1998*, notably Arthur's *and* his son's Right to Privacy in Family Life.

*   The seriousness of the assault.

*   Whether injuries have been inflicted on other occasions.

*   The vulnerability of the older person.

*   The availability of other carers, including residential facilities.

*   Acting in the best interests of the vulnerable adult.

Supporting carers

Again assuming no local Policy and Guidance exists, imagine that you decide to investigate further, being mindful of the concerns we have just identified.

It then transpires that the son has assaulted Arthur, but Arthur:

- Is continually wandering out of the home.

- Is prone to bouts of temper when he shouts abuse and throws objects.

- His son has had to give up work to stay at home to care for him and only gets a couple of hours a week to himself when his sister calls on Sunday lunch to give him a break.

It now begins to emerge that this isn't a simple abuser and victim situation, but rather a much more complex human relationship between an older person whose health is deteriorating and a loving son who has tolerated much abuse and made a personal sacrifice out of love for his father.

One potential way forward is to attempt to persuade the service user to undergo an assessment of need (S47(1) *NHSCCA, 1990*) and then see if you can persuade the son to have a similar assessment as a carer.

1. The son may also be assessed in his own right under S47(1) *NHSCCA 1990* as a result of the *Carers (Recognition and Services) Act 1995*. Since April 2001 his father does *not* have to ask for his own needs to be assessed for this to take place.

2. The son may be under great strain as a carer, and by identifying the need to give him brief breaks, you may be providing a safety valve. In essence, the bond between father and son maybe a loving one, but the continual pressure of care is causing him to 'lash out'. The breaks may remove the pressure and thereby *prevent* future assaults.

Clearly, *No Secrets* makes it much easier to respond since:

- Procedures are now in place (and thereby you will feel less 'on your own').

and

- The joint investigation team will be established to determine what action is appropriate both for the person who has been abused and for the son as the primary carer.

Sadly, however, you will encounter many similar situations where the relationship is abusive and cannot be remedied in this way.

Criminal violence

In deciding what to do in cases of criminal violence towards vulnerable adults, you will need to consider the following questions.

- Does the vulnerable adult have capacity?

- Is the service user at serious risk of future harm? Do I need to take preventative action now? Can I take preventative action?

- Does the situation warrant a police investigation? (The police have powers under Section 5(3) *PACE 1984* to arrest someone to protect a vulnerable adult but remember that common assault is *not* an arrestable offence.)

- Should the vulnerable adult be removed from home as a way of offering them protection if it is proven they lack capacity?

- There are new criminal offences of willful neglect and ill-treatment of a vulnerable adult as a result of Section 44, *MCA 2005*.

By now you should be making connections with the notion of domestic violence and the issues and tensions it poses for practice. The situations are quite similar. In reality, it appears to be easier to remove the victim than it is to deal with the aggressor.

Activity 3.4

This activity should take you about 15 minutes to complete.

Why do you think *No Secrets* stops short of imposing a legal duty on authorities to protect vulnerable adults?

Write down your views.

Comment

We suspect you found this a really difficult activity to complete.

Do you remember in the last activity you visited a vulnerable adult with severe bruising? The problem is that the service user has the right to say 'No thank you. I don't want anything to be done':

   unless it were ascertained that they lacked capacity.

In practice, all agencies have to walk a fine line between protecting a vulnerable person from abuse whilst not themselves being abusive by taking draconian action.

The Mental Capacity Act 2005 clarifies that everyone who is involved with vulnerable adults must always:

   act in the 'best interests' of the vulnerable adult.

and recently new safeguards have been introduced in the *Mental Health Act 2007* whenever it is being considered to deprive a person of their liberty who lacks capacity.

Review Activity

This activity should take you about 15 minutes to complete.

From what you have learnt in this session, identify the two potential types of legal error you could make in practice.

Comment

The problem for everyone who seeks to safeguard vulnerable adults is that potentially you can be:

- Damned if you don't.

You must not leave a vulnerable person who lacks capacity at risk of serious harm, and

- Damned if you do.

You must not act against the express wishes of the vulnerable adult who has capacity.

Clearly, capacity is a pivotal concept here and one worthy of further exploration, but for now we will look at the different settings in which abuse can take place.

Session Four: Where Can Abuse Take Place?

Session objectives

Upon completing this session you should be able to:

- Identify where abuse is likely to take place.

- Describe the procedures already in place for investigating certain types of abuse and complaints.

- Pin-point gaps in current provisions to protect vulnerable adults.

Introduction

The abuse of vulnerable adults can take place almost anywhere. The most obvious which spring to mind are:

- in a residential care home

- in a nursing home

- in a hospital

- at a day centre

- in their own home.

No Secrets asserts that the **perpetrator** (the person being abusive) could be:

- *a member of staff, proprietor or service manager*

- *a member of a recognised professional group*

- *a volunteer or member of a community group such as a place of worship or social club*

- *another service user*

- *a spouse, relative or member of the person's social network*

- *a carer, i.e. someone who is eligible for assessment under the Carers (Recognition and Services) Act 1995*

- *a neighbour, member of the public or stranger*

or

- *a person who deliberately targets vulnerable people in order to exploit them.*

(No Secrets, op cit: 11)

The following activity is designed to help you think about this further.

Activity 4.1

This activity should take you about 10 minutes to complete.

In the light of what you have just learnt about where abuse can occur, write down those areas which you believe are already covered and those you think will need to be covered by new procedures and protocols.

Comment

You probably began by grouping the list of perpetrators we've just seen in *No Secrets* and stated that those which are:

- work-related are already covered by the *Care Standards Act 2000*

and those which are:

- home or community based are not likely to be covered unless the abuse is by a professional worker or someone employed by an agency.

Work related abuse

Health and Social Services are bound by Common Law to abide by the:

> *General Duty of Care.*

This forms the basis of liability from which both civil claims and sometimes criminal charges can be brought.

The General Duty of Care means the Health Trust or Social Care Department could be sued if:

- It were to do something it should not have done (Breach Article 8 of the *HRA 1998* immediately springs to mind as an example).

or

- Failed to do something it should have done (i.e. behaved negligently).

To protect themselves from legal claims, agencies set up Procedures and Practices, including Disciplinary Procedures and Complaints Procedures.

Dimond (2004) identified four key areas in which health and social care professionals face accountability:

- civil law
- criminal law
- employment law
- professional registration (applies to Health and Social Care)

A number of areas which could attract liability quickly spring to mind, for example, with regard to health:

Where treatment is given without consent and there is no legal justification, then this would be a trespass to the person and gives a right of action for compensation in the civil courts.

(Dimond, 2004: 16)

Malpractice is not only the concern of civil law as:

. . . in extreme cases, there may also be criminal implications.

(Montgomery, 2003)

The acid test is:

. . . there must have been not merely negligence, but gross negligence.

(Montgomery, 2003: 188)

The criteria for establishing gross negligence are:

- Showing an obvious indifference.
- Being aware of risk, but deciding to ignore it.
- Attempting to avoid a risk but were so grossly negligent that it is considered punishment deserved.
- Giving inattention or failing to avert a serious risk, which goes beyond inadvertence.

To help you to link the law to practice we provide you with a practical activity.

Activity 4.2

Obtain a copy of your employer's disciplinary procedures.

Ensure you are clear about what you should do, what you shouldn't do, the limits of your authority and the rights of service users or patients to complain about specific matters.

Comment

By reminding yourselves of these procedures you should begin to see how and when liabilities can occur and of the importance of:

- Protecting vulnerable adults effectively.

whilst, at the same time:

- Not infringing their rights under the *Human Rights Act 1998*.

Para 2.17 of *No Secrets* lists different patterns of abuse. We will now replicate these, but would like you to check which ones you think *are already* covered by procedures and which aspects you believe *need to be addressed*.

1. **Serial abusing** whereby the perpetrator 'grooms' vulnerable people.

2. **Long-term abuse** in an on-going **family** relationship.

3. **Opportunistic abuse**, such as theft occurring because money has been left around.

4. **Situational abuse** where pressures have been built up or because of difficult or challenging behaviour.

5. **Neglect** because the carer has problems such as debt, alcohol abuse or mental ill health.

6. **Institutional abuse** which features poor care standards, lack of positive responses to complex needs, rigid routines, inadequate staffing and an insufficient knowledge base within the service.

7. **Unacceptable 'treatments' or programmes** such as sanctions, withholding food and drink, seclusion, unnecessary and unauthorised use of control and restraint or over-medication.

8. **Lack of appropriate guidance** on anti-racist and anti-discriminatory practice.

9. **Failure to access key services** such as health care, dentistry or prostheses.

10. **Misappropriation of benefits or other money** by other members of the household.

11. **Fraud or intimidation** in connection with wills, property or other assets.

(Adapted from *No Secrets*: 12)

We believe that:

- 6, 7, 8 and 9 are currently covered entirely by agencies' policies and should be addressed by the CSCI.

- 1, 3 and 11 can occur in the work setting *or* in a service user's own home.

- 2, 4, 5 and 10 are the challenges which arise as a result of *No Secrets* and form the nub of the Policy Group's work.

Before attempting to 'close the gaps' it might be helpful first to remind ourselves about the *Care Standards Act 2000* and the role played by the Care Quality Commission (CQC).

The *Care Standards Act 2000*

Section 6 of the *Care Standards Act 2000* establishes the *National Care Standards Commission* to be responsible for the:

> . . . *regulation of the whole range of care services from care homes for the elderly, children's homes, domiciliary care, fostering and adoption agencies through to independent hospitals, clinics, medical agencies and nursing agencies.*

The NCSC essentially took over the regulation and inspection functions created the *Registered Homes Act 1984*. It then merged with the Department of Health Inspectorate to become CSCI and in the near future will incorporate Health Authority responsibilities and become the Care Quality Commission.

Section 7 outlines 'Part II services', which include:

- Monitoring the availability and quality of services.
- Supporting consumers through the provision of information.
- Encouraging the development of better services.

by identifying 38 National Minimum Standards.

Sections 11 to 20 of the *CSA 2000* set out the procedures that underpin the registration process, the registration authorities day-to-day activities of:

- Considering applications.
- Conditions of registration.
- Cancellation of registration.
- Procedures for notifying applicants or providers of decisions.

Section 21 provides for the right of appeal.

National Minimum Standards

We have already learnt that 38 National Minimum Standards have been devised. For our present purpose the following are most relevant:

Standard 17 is set to ensure that:

Service users have their legal rights protected and are enabled to exercise these directly and participate in the civil process if they wish. Where the service user lacks capacity, the registered person should facilitate access to available advocacy services.

Standard 18 deals with protection whereby:

18.1   The registered person ensures that service users are safeguarded from physical, financial or material, psychological or sexual abuse, neglect, discriminatory abuse or self-harm, inhuman or degrading treatment, through deliberate intent, negligence or ignorance, in accordance with written policies.

18.2   Robust procedures for responding to suspicion or evidence of abuse or neglect (including whistle blowing) ensure the safety and protection of service users, including passing on concerns to the Care Standards Commission Inspectorate in accordance with the *Public Interest Disclosure Acts 1998* and *2004*, and the Department of Health (DoH) guidance *No Secrets*.

18.3   All allegations and incidents of abuse must be followed up promptly and action taken recorded.

Furthermore, Section 81, *CSA 2000* requires the Secretary of State to establish and maintain a list of individuals unsuitable to work with vulnerable adults, the Protection of Vulnerable Adults (POVA) list, whilst Section 82 imposes a duty on those who work with vulnerable adults to refer to the POVA list and a *duty* to refer care workers who have harmed, or placed a vulnerable adult at risk of harm, to the Secretary of State for inclusion on the POVA list.

The *Safeguarding Vulnerable Groups Act 2006*

The new *Safeguarding Vulnerable Groups Act 2006* has introduced a new legal requirement whereby anyone working, or volunteering to work, with vulnerable people, *must* be:

registered with the Independent Safeguarding Authority (ISA) as being a fit and suitable person.

It becomes an offence for a person to work or volunteer with vulnerable people if they are not registered and an offence for an organisation to employ or to allow them a non-registered person routine access to vulnerable people.

Under Section 59, the *SVGA 2006* introduces a new legal definition of vulnerable people whereby:

Vulnerability is considered to be something anyone might experience whenever they are in a situation where another person can exercise power, in the form of legitimate authority, over them.

Activity 4.3

This activity should take about 15 minutes to complete.

Write down a day-to-day situation in which someone may have legitimate authority over you.

Comment

The most obvious example would be going to hospital for treatment. Whilst you are in attendance those who have a general duty of care to you also can be viewed as having power over you even though assessment or treatment should only be given with your prior consent.

Below is the full list as shown under Section 59 but you should note well that at present this definition is only to be used when working under *Safeguarding Vulnerable Groups Act 2006* and the narrower definition you learnt in Session One arising out of *No Secrets* should be used in all other circumstances.

Under Section 59 and article 3 of the *SVGA Act*, a vulnerable adult is someone over 18 who:

(a) Is living in residential accommodation, such as a care home or a residential special school.

(b) Is living in sheltered housing.

(c) Is receiving domiciliary care in their own home.

(d) Is receiving any form of health care.

(e) Is detained in a prison, remand centre, young offender institution, secure training centre or attendance centre.

(f) Is in contact with probation services.

(g) Is receiving a welfare service of a description to be prescribed in regulations.

(h) Is receiving a service or participating in an activity which is specifically targeted at people with age-related needs, disabilities or prescribed physical or mental health conditions or expectant or nursing mothers living in residential care (age-related needs includes needs associated with frailty, illness, disability or mental capacity).

(i) Is receiving direct payments from a local authority/HSS body in lieu of social care services.

(j) Requires assistance in the conduct of their own affairs.

The Guidance to the Act adds that the key here is that:

In all the above settings and situations adults need to be able to trust the people caring for them, supporting them and/or providing them with services.

Having looked at vulnerability we will now look at how the quality of service is guaranteed and what happens when a service falls below an acceptable level.

Quality assurance and complaints

Section 48(1) of the *NHSCCA 1990* requires that premises used for the provision of community care must be registered and inspected in accordance with procedure laid down in:

- Part II of the *Care Standards Act 2000*.

Section 3 of the *CSA 2000* defines a care home as:

Any home which provides accommodation together with nursing or personal care for any person who is, or has been ill (including mental disorder), is disabled or infirm, or who has a dependence on drugs or alcohol.

Section 50 requires the local authority to devise a complaints procedure and to publicise it widely. Complaints may be made about any community care service or treatment in a residential establishment, whether run by the local authority, by a voluntary organisation or by a privately run company.

Activity 4.4

This activity should take about 15 minutes to complete.

Obtain a copy of the complaints procedure that operates in your area. Read it through and ask yourself the following questions.

- Is it written in a clear style?
- Is it available in other languages?
- Does it inform the service user how the complaint will be dealt with, and how the service user will be informed of the outcome?

Comment

By asking yourself these questions you will be appraising accessibility and the appropriateness of the complaints procedure.

Complaints may be made under Section 78 of the *Local Authority Social Services Act 1970*, as defined under Section 50 of the *NHSCCA 1990*. This allows people to complain:

- About the quality of services provided.
- That they have not been assessed as needing a service.

In cases of maladministration, complaints may be made to the local government ombudsman, but this must be within 12 months.

Complainants may, further:

- Seek legal advice to see if they can sue the council for a breach of its statutory duty (but this may be difficult to prove).
- Ask for judicial review of the council's decision or action in the High Court.
- Report the council to the Secretary of State for Health under Section 50, *NHSCCA 1990* if they think that 'the council has a duty to provide a service it will not provide or that it unfairly withdrew that service'.

Inspection and investigation

As CSCI has both powers and duties to inspect premises, ensure the safety of residents and investigate suspected malpractice and abuse, it is essential that everyone working with vulnerable adults is aware of the need to report any concerns to them.

One local Inter-Agency Policy, Procedure and Practice Guidance states that if a referral concerns a person in a facility registered by CSCI including:

- care homes
- nursing agencies
- domiciliary care

then:

> *The Inspectorate must be informed immediately so that the provider complies with their statutory responsibilities under the Care Standards Act 2000.*

> (Section 11: 1 of 2)

This requirement reflects the recognition that should one person be experiencing abuse by a statutory provider, it is highly likely that others will also be at risk. CSCI's powers and duties are wide ranging as in:

Section 31(2) which deals with inspection of premises:

> *A person authorised by the registration authority may at any time enter and inspect premises which are used, or which he has reasonable cause to believe to be used, as an establishment or for the purposes of an agency.*

- Under Section 31(4) documents and records may be seized.

- Under Section 31(3) inspectors may interview in private any person employed there, and, with consent, *'any patient or person accommodated or cared for there'.*

Interviews *must* be conducted in accordance with Codes Band C of *PACE 1984*. Furthermore, a medical practitioner or medical nurse authorised by CSCI who has *'reasonable cause to believe that a patient or person accommodated or cared for there is not receiving proper care'*, can, with consent, *'examine him in private and inspect any medical records relating to his treatment in the establishment'.* ('Him' above stands for 'her and him'.)

It is an offence to intentionally obstruct anyone exercising these powers.

As CSCI has strong powers and adult protection teams do not, it seems quite staggering they appear to be pushing the responsibility of protection in care homes and registered community care facilities onto local authorities.

Review Activity

Meena Ghoshi's daughter has complained that some of the staff at Holyoaks Care Home are verbally abusive to Meena and many of the other residents. These staff members are disrespectful and openly express the view that old people aren't any good to anyone.

Write down what you should do and what you believe might happen.

Comment

You should bring this matter to the attention of the adult protection team who in turn should raise the matter with CSCI. As we have learnt earlier, although e CSCI has the powers to investigate, they are likely to ask the local authority to conduct the initial investigation.

The adult protection co-ordinator visits Holyoaks to see the manager. The manager is full of platitudes and re-assurances, but no concrete action is proposed.

We would have expected the manager to conduct a full internal investigation as these matters are serious. Clearly, some staff, if the claim is true, do not meet the GSCC's Code of Conduct or Values Requirements and should be deemed:

unfit to practice.

From September 2008 due consideration should be given to consulting with the Independent Safeguarding Authority to see whether the individual should lose their status as a 'fit person' to work with vulnerable adults.

If the complaint had been about physical or financial abuse we would have expected the manager to immediately suspend the staff involved and many believe this should happen here.

It is important that the adult protection co-ordinator puts pressure on CSCI to take this up as poor management and therefore as a serious concern about the home.

CSCI has powers to address concerns and make a visit to discuss the home's continuing eligibility for registration. Section 31(5) requires CSCI to prepare a report on the matters inspected and send copies to each person registered in respect of the establishment or agency.

If the circumstances required urgent action Section 20 allows CSCI to apply to a justice of the peace for an Order to:

1. Cancel the registration of a person in respect of an establishment or agency.

2. Vary or remove any condition for the time being.

3. Impose an additional condition.

Registration could also be cancelled routinely under:

> The 'normal procedure' defined under Section 14, CSA 2000.

One important issue does, however, still need to be addressed, as private care homes fall outside of the *Human Rights Act 1998*. Pressure groups are seeking to have this amended in the Health and Social Care Bill claiming some older people are forced to wear incontinence pads as staff do not have the time to take them to the toilet and others are over-medicated to keep them docile. It is our view this is not a Human Rights issue alone, but rather one where CSCI *already* has sufficient powers to address such concerns, if only it had the will to do so.

In this session we have seen that abuse can occur in a variety of locations. Strong legal protection is available in community care facilities and care homes if people are prepared to use them, but investigation and protection in the person's own home is much more problematic.

Session Five: Consolidating the Issues and Setting the Agenda for Implementation

Session objectives

Upon completing this session you should be able to:

- Have awareness of the challenges presented by the implementation of *No Secrets*.

- Identify ways in which you can contribute.

- Confirm your understanding of the various kinds of abuse which can occur.

- Explain the role of the multi-agency management committee and the vulnerable adults protection team.

- Outline why investigation procedures are necessary.

Introduction

We have already learnt that *No Secrets* requires all agencies to be aware of a variety of forms of abuse, which vulnerable adults can experience in a variety of settings.

We have also looked at the need to:

- Protect vulnerable people from abuse.

but not at the expense of:

- Their Rights under the *Human Rights Act 1998*.

This dilemma is such a difficult one to address that the Government decided not to introduce new legislation and the Notes of Guidance, Statutory Instruments and other Circulars which goes with new law, but rather chose instead to heighten awareness of abuse through *No Secrets* which is, in effect, 'Policy Guidance'.

We have also seen that vulnerable people should already be protected when they live in hospitals, residential care homes and nursing homes and from abuse by those providing community care services. That said, we must never be complacent, and health and local authorities should regularly review their mechanisms for inspection, investigating complaints and the disciplinary code used to tackle staff suspected of abusive behaviour.

The main new business for local Policy Developers has thus centred around:

- Protecting vulnerable adults from abuse in their own homes.

- Protecting vulnerable adults from abuse by other parties in the community.

And this is a challenge we will now explore.

The challenge

The challenge for everyone who works with vulnerable adults is to ensure we offer better protection without infringing anyone's rights. We have an important part to play by:

- *Contributing* to the debate by sharing our own practice experiences.

- *Ensuring* our knowledge is current and relevant.

- *Revisiting* the value base of our practice to check our commitment to eradicate oppression and maltreatment.

- *Being aware* of the tasks of the multi-agency management committee and being alert to the sound reasoning behind the principles it will have to juggle to ensure fairness to all.

- *Co-operating* with the vulnerable adults investigation team once established so we can all develop by improving practice.

- *Ensuring* our approach is *balanced*, thereby avoiding potential errors of omission and commission.

The process begins with a p*olicy and service audit* in order to:

> . . . *evaluate the way in which policies, procedures and practices for the protection of vulnerable adults are working.*

(op cit: 18)

To ensure *every perspective* is addressed, the approach must be a multi-agency one, and we have already seen why the membership of the management group should be diverse (this list was reproduced earlier in this workbook).

No Secrets states that the audit process *must* incorporate eight core elements:

- *An evaluation of community understanding – the extent to which there is an awareness of the policy and procedures for protecting vulnerable adults.*

- *Links with other systems for protecting those at risk, for example, child protection, domestic violence, victim support and community safety.*

- *An evaluation of how agencies are working together and how far the policy continues to be appropriate.*

- *The extent to which operational guidance continues to be appropriate in general and, in the light of reported cases of abuse, in particular.*

- *The training available to staff of all agencies.*

- *The performance and quality of services for the protection of vulnerable adults.*

- *The conduct of investigations in individual cases.*

- *The development of services to respond to the needs of adults who have been abused.*

Activity 5.1

This activity should take you about 15 minutes to complete.

From your experience, and from what you have learnt in this workbook write down what you believe is necessary before setting up an investigation team and some suggestions as to what the investigation might cover.

Comment

This activity was designed to reflect how important *you* are in making *No Secrets* work effectively in practice.

Many people will have thought the starting point is to:

> *. . . ensure that everyone at the operational level understands the inter-agency policies and procedures, know their own role and have access to comprehensive guidance.*

(op cit: 26)

It is precisely these aspects which have made Area Child Protection Committees (ACPCs) an over-whelming success.

You probably thought that the investigation of an *individual* matter will need a 'framework' but this should be flexible and fluid enough to be adapted to meet specific needs.

Issues in defining abuse

In order to devise such a framework it is important to be clear as to what behaviour may or may not be defined as abuse. To help move us on Leveridge (2001; 2007) has raised four important questions which need to be addressed within the context of working with vulnerable adults.

1. When does 'care' become 'control', and 'control' become 'abuse'?

2. Should we separate, and deal separately with, intentional and unintentional abuse?

3. How far should we take account of the interactional effects in a specific situation, such as stress?

4. When does the lack of services, or the provision of inappropriate services, constitute a form of abuse?

These questions mean the context of adult investigation work will be far more wide-ranging than in child protection which has its own clearly defined checklist.

Adult abuse

One set of local Inter-agency Policy, Procedures and Practice Guidance defines abuse and mistreatment as:

> . . . *behaviour that may cause significant harm or results in the serious exploitation of a vulnerable adult. Abuse is a violation of an individual's human and civil rights by another person or persons.*

In Session 1 we got you to think about the main forms of abuse and pinpointed the six main areas addressed in *No Secrets*. We now reproduce these, with a little more explanation:

1. *Physical abuse*
    This includes hitting, slapping, pushing, kicking, misuse of medication, restraint or inappropriate sanctions.

2. *Sexual abuse*
    This includes rape and sexual assault or sexual acts to which the vulnerable adult has not consented, or could not consent, or was pressurised into consenting.

3. *Psychological abuse*
    This includes emotional abuse, threats of harm or abandonment, deprivation of contact, humiliation, blaming, controlling, intimidation, coercion, harassment, verbal abuse, isolation, or withdrawal from services or supportive networks.

4. *Financial or material abuse*
    This includes theft, fraud, exploitation, pressure in connection with making a Will, property or inheritance or financial transactions, or the misuse of misappropriation of property, possessions or benefits.

5. *Neglect and acts of omission*
    This includes ignoring medical or physical care needs, failure to provide access to appropriate health care, social care or educational services, the withholding of the necessities of life, such as medication, adequate nutrition and heating.

6. *Discriminatory abuse*
    This includes racist, sexist and other actions that are based on a person's disability, and other forms of harassment, slurs, or similar treatment.

Any or all of these types of abuse may be perpetrated as a result of deliberate intent, negligence or ignorance. Incidents may be multiple, either against one person in a continuing relationship or service context, or against more than one person at a time.

N.B. You will be expected to be aware of the main signs and symptoms of the various forms of abuse and should consult the toolkit found in most local authorities' published guidance.

Investigating adult abuse

No Secrets requires the objectives of an adult abuse investigation to be wide-ranging and will cover aspects such as:

- Establishing the facts.

- Assessing the needs of vulnerable adults for protection, support and redress.

- Making decisions with regard to what follow-up action should be taken with regard to:
  – the perpetrator
  – the service or its management if they have been
    ○ culpable
    ○ ineffective
    ○ negligent.

Whilst it is possible criminal proceedings could follow, this is not always the case. What is important is that:

All those making a complaint or allegation or expressing concern, whether they be staff, service users, carers or members of the general public, should be reassured that:

- *They will be taken seriously.*

- *Their comments will be treated confidentially, but their concerns may be shared if they or others are at significant risk.*

- *If service users, they will be given immediate protection from risk of reprisals or intimidation.*

- *If staff, they will be afforded protection if necessary, e.g. under the Public Interest Disclosure Acts 1998 and 2004.*

- *They will be dealt with in a fair and equitable manner.*

- *They will be kept informed of action that has been taken and its outcome.*

Investigative procedures

Prior to *No Secrets* investigation was at best *patchy* and usually only took place in the most extreme cases. Here is an activity to illustrate the point based on the author's actual experience.

Activity 5.2

Once I supervised a student on a Hospital Social Work placement. She was concerned because the adult son of an elderly female patient used to arrive every evening at 7.30 to visit and would bring with him a large bag of barley sugar sweets.

The problem was his mother was very wealthy, but more significantly, was diabetic.

Although the hospital stopped his visits the student was frequently taunted with unkind jibes by the nurses. Write down how you feel about the incident.

Comment

Personally, I cannot find anything vaguely amusing about someone attempting to murder someone, no matter how benignly this is done. The son obviously knew of his mother's diabetes and this appears to have been a pre-meditated decision, callously executed, and, to compound matters, done in such a way that he might be able to avoid blame by tapping into some people's strange (and dangerous) sense of humour.

Although different professional groups are prone to react in different ways to the same presenting issues, in this instance the reaction of a couple of individual nurses was transparently inappropriate given the actual seriousness of the incident. I feel the son should have been prosecuted and not just banned from visiting and I also believe the patient's finances should have been protected.

No Secrets requires local authorities to produce a framework within which all concerned with vulnerable adults at an operational level must practice. The first priority is to:

> *ensure the protection and safety of vulnerable adults*

requiring:

> *all staff to take responsibility to act on any suspicion of abuse or neglect.*

One local Policy and Practice Guidance recognises at the outset a number of key principles which underpin sound practice:

- *Actively work together* within the inter-agency framework.

- *Actively promote* the empowerment and well-being of vulnerable adults through the service they provide.

- *Act in a way which supports the rights of the individual* to lead an independent life based on self determination and personal choice.

- *Recognise people who are unable to take their own decisions* and/or protect themselves, their assets and bodily integrity, i.e. physical, financial or sexual abuse.

- *Recognise that the right to self-determination can involve risk* and ensure that such risk is recognised and understood by all concerned and minimised whenever possible (there should be on open discussion between the individual and the agencies about the risks involved to thrm).

- *Ensure the safety of vulnerable adults* by integrating strategies, policies and services relevant to abuse within the framework of the *NHS and Community Care Act 1990*, the *Mental Health Act 1983*, the *Public Interest Disclosure Act 1998*, the *Care Standards Act 2000*, the *Human Rights Act 1998* and the *Data Protection Act 1998*, and, of course, the *Mental Capacity Act 2005*.

- *Ensure that when the right to an independent lifestyle and choice is at risk the individual concerned receives appropriate help*, including advice, protection and support from relevant agencies.

- *Ensure that the law and statutory requirements are known and used appropriately* so that vulnerable adults receive the protection of the law and access to the judicial process.

- *Respect the rights of the alleged perpetrator.*

Furthermore, Procedures and Guidance should lay down key aspects to ensure the involvement of the vulnerable adult, notably:

- The involvement of the adult should be enabled throughout the procedure from the time of referral. In some cases, it will be necessary to appoint an Independent Advocate to support or represent the interests of the person who is suspected of being abused.

- The protection of the vulnerable adult should be paramount when undertaking any adult protection enquiry. It is important to ensure that language and cultural issues are recognised and addressed through specialist advice and interpreters. It is equally important to have the assistance of an interpreter of British Sign Language and Makaton for the vulnerable adult when this is their first means of communication.

- The assessment process should maintain a focus on the needs of the individual adult. It should always include consideration of the way religious beliefs and cultural traditions in different racial, ethnic and cultural groups influence their values, attitudes and behaviour and the way in which family and community life is structured and organised. Cultural factors neither explain nor condone acts of omission or commission that place an adult at risk of significant harm.

- When undertaking an Adult Protection Enquiry it is important to respect the right of vulnerable people to take decisions with regard to their own safety. Vulnerable people should, therefore, be enabled, encouraged and supported to take the decisions, which they are able to take.

Some initial thoughts about capacity

The general principle has always been:

the wishes of the service user to have no action taken should not *be over-ridden as long as they are able to give* informed consent.

It is reassuring that *No Secrets* recognises capacity as perhaps being the key issue to be addressed:

The vulnerable adult's capacity is the key to action since if someone has 'capacity' and declines assistance this limits the help he or she may be given.

(op cit: 31)

Para 6.21 further adds:

In order to make sound decisions, the vulnerable adult's emotional, physical, intellectual and mental capacity in relation to self-determination and consent and any intimidation, misuse of authority or undue influence will have to be addressed.

(31)

This latter statement clearly supports the former, but sandwiched between these sentences is an even greater challenge. If the vulnerable adult declines assistance:

It will not however limit the action that may be required to protect others who are at risk of harm.

We can only presume this means:

- If the allegation is about the conduct of staff, further action can be taken *regardless* of the individuals desire not to proceed.

- If the allegation is about a carer, relative or friend the Guidance *implies* this gives a cause for concern about others living in the home, or in the home of the alleged abuser.

If my interpretation is correct, the second point will require much painstaking thought to avoid the dilemma of taking effective action whilst respecting the rights of individuals and the right to privacy in family life.

However, in spite of the challenges the implementation of *No Secrets* presents it is important to remind ourselves of people like the woman with diabetes who *are* vulnerable and who rely on us for protection.

No Secrets is equally positive in what should be the outcome of the investigation and assessment, namely, an agreed plan of action which sets out:

- *What steps are to be taken to assure his or her safety in the future.*

- *What treatment or therapy he or she can access.*

- *Modifications in the way services are provided (e.g. same gender care or placement).*

- *How best to support the individual through any action he or she takes to seek justice or redress.*

- *Any on-going risk management strategy required where this is deemed appropriate.*

(op cit: 32)

Activity 5.3

This activity should take you about 15 minutes to complete.

Think about potential areas of abuse vulnerable people might experience in the area of practice in which you are currently employed.

Now ask yourself:

1.   Do I take time to go beyond the superficial to see how service users really are and what they're really feeling?

2.   If I get an uncomfortable feeling do I probe a little, tell someone else or turn to the next task?

3.   If I had a concern would I know who to go to for advice?

4.   Do I feel it's not really my business when I'm in someone else's home?

Comment

At this point it is absolutely crucial if you haven't already done so, that you obtain the Inter-Agency Policy, Procedures and Practice Guidance and use this as your point of reference.

Let us now attempt to answer each of the four questions ensuring consistency with this document as far as is practicable.

1.   As you are likely to be the person making an initial referral it is important you have *'reasonable grounds'* for raising a concern. It is vital that you do spend a few minutes checking out your suspicions or verifying the claim, but it is equally important that you:
     - Do *not* ask leading questions.

nor

     - Go into any detail which may later become important as a potential piece of evidence. Effectively you must avoid contaminating evidence in case the matter proceeds to court or you could become in breach of the *sub-judice* rules.

2.   Once you have a strong feeling there is, or has been, abuse, you need to share your concerns with your line manager as soon as possible.

3.   Any concerns should be reported *immediately* to your line manager who will make an immediate referral to adult protection if they believe there is sufficient evidence to warrant a formal investigation.

4. It is not just 'your business', its your *duty* to check out concerns (within the parameters already outlined) and report the matter.

The Guiding Principle is to be found in Section 2, page1:

All agencies undertake to respond promptly to situations that indicate that a vulnerable adult is being mistreated and to respond sensitively to the needs and rights of the individual taking account of his/her racial and cultural background, gender, religious belief, sexuality, age and disability.

Activity 5.4

This activity should take you about 15 minutes to complete.

You receive an anonymous phone call in the social services duty team to say that Rhandiner Khan, a 73-year-old woman has been assaulted by her 51-year-old son.

Write down why you think you need to consult with your line manager before informing the police or taking other formal action.

Comment

It is an established fact that racists have used child protection as a vehicle to intimidate people from ethnic minority communities and we need to be alert that the anonymous phone call is not in a similar vein. (Haluk Soyden of the University of Orebrau, Sweden has conducted an excellent survey of responses made by Swedish and Leicester social workers if you wish to explore this issue further.)

So we need to act swiftly to protect, where appropriate, but we also need to act sensitively and in the way we respect other people's rights.

Your line manager may well be aware of any previous incidents where there have been unfounded and malicious allegations. Checking out needs to happen swiftly but it is an important part of the investigative process. If your line manager believes further action is warranted a strategy meeting will be convened.

Review Activity

At this point it is necessary to check out your own understanding of the key issues.

1. Am I aware of the symptoms of the six main forms of abuse?

2. Am I aware of the limits placed on me by law under the *Human Rights Act 1998*?

3. Have I read the Inter-Agency Policy, Procedures and Practice Guidelines?

4. Am I clear as to how far I can check out a concern before it needs to be passed on?

5. Am I clear as to the investigative process and of the role of strategy meetings?

Comment

We hope you are clear on the first four questions but you may be less clear on the fifth.

Strategy meetings

The purpose of the strategy meeting is to plan a detailed response in respect of the concern(s) raised and agree what action is required to protect the vulnerable adult.

The meeting will identify which agency/agencies will be involved in any investigation. The action considered will be in four areas:

1. Single agency investigation

The investigating agency will be any agency represented at the discussion/meeting and the Investigating Officer will be named.

2. Joint agency investigation

The investigating agencies will be identified. The Investigating Officers will be named.

The following should be determined at the strategy meeting:

- Clarify the responsibilities of the investigating officer(s).

- Agree an adult protection plan.

- Make arrangements for the next discussion/meeting that must take place within one calendar month.

3. Assessment and/or support

The meeting may have identified that there is a need for assessment or support and this remains within the *No Secrets* procedures.

4. No further action

The meeting may have decided there are no protection concerns under the *No Secrets* procedures. However, a decision may be made to recommend that a Community Care Assessment be carried out under Section 47(1) *NHSCCA 1990*, and Section 47(2) if the person meets the criteria of being disabled as defined under Section 29 of the *NAA 1948*.

One important development brought about by the Protection of Vulnerable Adults (POVA) is that many local authorities have now modified their FACS criteria (Fairer Access to Care Services) so that individuals may now be placed in one of the four categories.

- critical
- substantial
- medium
- low

according to the level of *risk* presented to them as well as the level of *need*.

Session Six: Effective Practice, Risk and Harm Reduction

Session objectives

Upon completing this session you should be able to:

- Outline the key principles underpinning effective practice.

- Detail the key issues in assessing risk.

- Describe the range of outcomes that can follow from an initial concern.

Introduction

In this session we will look at:

- the principles behind effective practice

- risk

- capacity

- the range of outcomes that can result from an initial adult protection referral.

Principles of effective practice

There are six key principles to be addressed in developing practice guidance:

1. **To actively work together.**
   This requires not only information sharing but also establishing protocols as to how inter-agency working is to be achieved e.g. establishing an adult protection investigation team akin to child protection teams with agreed Guidance and Procedures underpinning practice.

2. **To support the rights of individuals.**
   Individual vulnerable people have the right to choose how they live and whether or not they require help or support, even if it is believed they are being subjected to any form of abuse.

3. **To recognise people who are unable to make their own decisions.**
   Some vulnerable adults do not have the mental capacity to make decisions for themselves. This has long been recognised with regard to financial matters. *No Secrets* now places a similar challenge on us to think about mental competence in relation to physical, emotional and sexual abuse.

4. **To recognise that the right to self-determination can involve risk.**
   Even when a vulnerable adult is deemed to be mentally competent and chooses to decline help, support and other forms of intervention it is important that we:

   ensure risk is recognised and understood by all concerned and minimised by sharing our concerns with others in open discussion (for example if we suspect a carer is being physically abusive to other service users).

5. **To ensure that the law and statutory requirements are known and that vulnerable adults are aware how to access the judicial process.**
   If the vulnerable adult is mentally competent, we should not only let the abusing person know of our concerns but also go beyond this and ensure the vulnerable adult is aware of their legal rights and entitlements.

6. **To provide effective support for the vulnerable adult throughout any court hearing.**
   This principle should have always been included as good practice, but since May 2002 has been carried forward into new legislation as you will see below.

The *Youth Justice and Criminal Evidence Act 1999*

The *Youth Justice and Criminal Evidence Act 1999* was passed to support:

   vulnerable witnesses and victims

in any legal hearing.

The main principles behind the Act have been translated into practice Guidance in the form of:

   Achieving Best Evidence in Criminal Proceedings: Guidance for Vulnerable or Intimidated Witnesses, including Children. Home Office/Lord Chancellor's Office/CPS/DOH, 2001.

Essentially, it has been recognised that vulnerable adults need more help to access justice than others.

Activity 6.1

This activity should take you about 15 minutes to complete.

You are working with Tammy Lane, a 33-year-old with a severe learning disability who claims to have been sexually assaulted by a man who lives at the end of her road.

Do you think Tammy will have additional problems when seeking help from the law than other women? Make a note of your thoughts.

Comment

You probably thought about how Tammy is going to get people to believe her. 'Normalisation' and 'inclusion' are fine words for social work, but those administering the law are more concerned about evidence and proof. Tammy's evidence will have to be convincing. She will face disbelieving interviews and is likely to be questioned about her disability and experts called to say how 'competent' she is to give testimony. Tammy will also be assessed as to how well she would be able to give her evidence and how well she will be able to stand up to cross-examination.

The *Youth Justice and Criminal Evidence Act 1999* recognises for the first time that some witnesses may be 'vulnerable' namely:

> *Those who have a disability or illness that the court considers is likely to affect the quality of their evidence.*

> (*Achieving Best Evidence in Criminal Proceedings*, Vol.1, 2002: 3)

As a result, 'Special Measures' have been introduced to assist such witnesses, as in the case of learning disabled witnesses, as a result of Section 16(2)(a)(ii) of the *YJCEA 1999*, namely:

- Screens to shield the witness from the defendant.

- A live link so the witness can give evidence during the trial from outside the court through a televised link to the courtroom.

- Giving evidence in private.

- Removal of wigs and gowns by judges and barristers.

- A video recorded interview may be admitted by the court as the witness' evidence in chief.

- Examination of the witness through an *intermediary*.

- Aids to communication to be provided.

- Mandatory protection of witness from cross-examination by the accused in person.

- Discretionary protection of witness from cross-examination by the accused in person.

- Restrictions on evidence and questions about the complainant's sexual behaviour.

Assessment of risk

Risk assessment is a two-way street. It looks at:

- risk *to* the individual

- risk to others *from* the individual.

We will deal with the second form first as it is probably less contentious.

Risk to others

Risk assessment is routinely addressed when working with:

- People who have committed a sexual or violent crime.

- Mentally disordered offenders.

- People with mental ill health whose condition has been deemed to be so serious as to warrant treatment in a secure environment.

The *Local Government Act 2003* recognised how important it is to identify the risks some people pose to others by establishing Multi-agency Public Protection Arrangements (MAPPA) to monitor 'dangerous' people in the name of public safety.

The *Mental Health Act, 2007* also recognises this by introducing Community Treatment Orders to be used with eligible discharged mental patients.

Risk from others

We are more likely to be involved with instances where it is believed somebody has abused a vulnerable adult. As part of assessing risk we need to ask:

What is the likelihood of the perpetrator repeating the abusive behaviour?

However, if the abuse is at home or in the community and having assessed risk, we are constrained as to what we can do.

We may in effect only intervene if:

- The victim wishes.

- A crime has been committed.

- The victim lacks capacity.

- You have reasonable cause to believe that the perpetrator will abuse other people.

The local Procedures and Practice Guidance produced should reflect these considerations by asking rhetorical questions such as:

- How vulnerable is the individual victim?

- What is the nature and extent of the abuse?

- What impact has the abuse had on the well-being of the victim?

- Is the abuse a one-off incident or part of a long standing or repeated pattern?

- Are other people being damaged, threatened, or at risk?

- Was the act deliberate, calculated or planned?

- Was the act against the law?

- Is the act likely to be repeated?

- Does the carer have generally good coping skills?

These questions help practitioners set an agenda to appraise risk objectively.

Activity 6.2

This activity should take you about 15 minutes to complete.

The law recognises that some factors make an offence more serious (aggravating factors) whilst others make the offence less serious (mitigating factors). The law also recognises motivation and intent.

Write down why you believe carers/family members/friends or neighbours may abuse a vulnerable person and then, using the considerations above, try to think what makes some situations more high risk than others.

Comment

Abuse can occur for a wide range of reasons.

The continual demands, both physical and emotional, can lead carers to breaking point. The carer becomes tired, exhausted, frustrated and left feeling unable to go on without help. The *Carers (Recognition and Services) Act 1995* allows carers to have their own needs assessed and for carers to be given periods of respite. Since April 2001, a carer can now ask for an assessment even if the person they care for is not seeking one. Dealing with this kind of abuse is quite straightforward as the carer is often full of guilt and remorse anyway and is usually relieved that professional workers are going to intervene in a supportive and non-judgemental manner.

Unfortunately, some abuse occurs because a person close to the vulnerable adult wishes to acquire their money or property, or acts out of malice. Such cases leave us feeling uncomfortable and frequently angry. If the victim is mentally competent and chooses not to accept help it can also lead to frustration as well. Safeguarding at least allows us to:

- Recognise that abuse has occurred.

- Inform the person behaving abusively that we are aware of their behaviour and alert to any recurrence.

- Share our feelings with others in a professional forum.

We also asked you to think about what makes some circumstances higher risk than others. The key elements seem to us to be:

1. **Seriousness:** There is a reason to believe someone's life or physical well being is in danger and that a serious crime may have been committed.

2. **Motivation:** The behaviour is calculated, deliberate and intentional.

3. **Frequency:** The behaviour is becoming more frequent.

4. **Intensity:** The behaviour is becoming more severe.

Within this framework it is important to remember, *regardless of where the abuse takes place, or by whom*, that:

> *repeated instances of poor care may also be an indicator of a more serious problem of abuse.*

Immediate protection

Although it is essential to provide immediate protection to vulnerable adults this should only be done in:

- Circumstances where the victim wishes such action, unless they lack competence.

- At immediate risk of serious harm.

It is essential that proper investigation and assessment take place *before* decisive action unless there is so clear cut a case that the public would expect the police to become involved.

Activity 6.3

This activity should take you about 10 minutes to complete.

Write down the dilemmas you face when acting in *an emergency*.

Comment

Your duties to vulnerable adults are, to some extent, ambiguous, as you need to:

- support and protect them

whilst at the same time you:

- do not infringe their rights.

It is also important you do not make ill-founded accusations against a third party in an attempt to safeguard.

Imagine you took the word of a service user that their son was about to murder them, only later to discover that their son had not been near the house for several weeks, and the service user was on the point of a psychotic breakdown. In such circumstances you might just find you need to defend yourself against:

> *a charge of defamation of character brought by the son.*

The reason we asked you to look at an emergency situation is that feelings can run high and hence you are more likely to act rashly and make a mistake. Your mistake may have been in 'good faith' but can still have very serious consequences.

One set of local Guidance and Procedure for Staff gives helpful advice by outlining procedures to be followed by staff in the event they suspect, or need to report, abuse of a vulnerable adult:

> *. . . who is or may be in need of community care services by reason of mental or other disability, age or illness and who is, or may be, unable to take control of him or herself or unable to protect him or herself against significant harm or exploitation.*

The duty of staff is to:

- Gather as much information as possible and record their concerns.

- Seek advice from the line manager *to ensure that any potential investigation is not compromised.*

Here, there is clear recognition that the key to effective intervention is finding out, recording and liasing to determine what needs to be done and to avoid challenges of inappropriate behaviour whilst *at the same time*:

> *. . . acting as quickly and expeditiously as possible to minimise risk to individuals.*

This is reflected in the overall Procedures and Practice Guidance where the Adult Protection Strategy meeting should take place within 24 hours of the referral. If the alleged abuse were in a registered care home, the manager should interview the staff member and:

> *suspend them pending a full investigation.*

This protects the vulnerable adult from recriminations and protects the 'evidence'. For that reason we cannot emphasise too strongly the assertion that *appropriate advice should be sought from Legal Services* whenever intervention is being considered.

Choosing to intervene

Common Law procedures allow those concerned about:

the welfare of a vulnerable person who lacks capacity to make an application to the Court of Protection for an Order of Declaratory Relief.

Schwehr (2002) explains:

The declaration can cover matters such as: where the person needs to live: whose company the person should have (and under what circumstances, e.g. supervision); and what the arrangements for personal care should be.

The declaration can even cover restraint, and in extreme circumstances, detention of the individual for their own safety, at least for a short period pending, for instance, completion of an investigation into the conduct of the client's carers, if there is an allegation of neglect.

(Schwehr, 2002; 18: 28)

The Declaration can ask for:

an emergency injunction, without notice to a relative suspected of abuse.

Schwehr adds there are two things needed to make such an application:

1. *A proposal* for the daily living arrangements for the person, about which there is a dispute – either with the person themselves, or the relatives or carers.

2. *Cogent evidence* as to the person's incapacity to make or communicate their own decision about the proposal.

Whilst it is indeed welcome that we appear to have acquired a mechanism *which is used carefully and appropriately* and enables adult protection teams to act when there are *serious* concerns about a vulnerable adults welfare who lacks capacity, it is potentially dangerous to adopt the view that:

. . . local authorities could theoretically face damages claims for not taking the steps which are now available.

(Schwehr, 2002, op cit: 29)

Before rushing into any application for a Declaration it would seem prudent to be certain that there is:

sufficient evidence that abuse is actually taking place.

Someone with, for instance, Alzheimer's, can easily believe other people are doing horrendous things to them but this may not be grounded in reality at all. This doesn't mean we dismiss all allegations of abuse but rather our practice must always:

adopt a balanced *approach and be tempered with common sense and self-restraint.*

Choosing not to intervene: offering support

Under the *Children Act 1989* the 'No Order' principle doesn't mean doing nothing, it means whenever possible we should work with people without recourse to statutory Orders.

Under *No Secrets* we may have a vulnerable adult who has capacity and clearly has been abused; here we have no right to intervene but we *can* offer support.

Women experiencing domestic violence *prior* to the *Family Law Act 1996* and the *Protection from Harassment Act 1997* often felt it was 'better to stay with the devil I know.' As professionals, we couldn't do anything about this officially, but good practitioners quickly formed new alliances. When visiting a woman who had experienced domestic violence, but wanted no formal intervention, the seasoned practitioner quickly learnt to give them the telephone number of the Women's Aid Helpline for:

- a fellow woman to talk to

- support

- legal advice if requested.

No Secrets should lead adult protection workers down the road of forming similar alliances with organisations such as 'Age Concern', until such time as the gap in the law is recognised and there is a willingness by Government to respond.

The decision to intervene or not intervene is not a simple one although we do have a number of Guiding Principles:

- If a person has capacity and doesn't wish it, we cannot intervene on their behalf.

- This doesn't preclude offering advice and support.

- If a person lacks capacity we could intervene but subject to
  – adequate proof that abuse is actually taking place.

But we should still in the first place:

- Attempt to work with the alleged perpetrator to resolve the matter and prevent recurrence rather than rush out for a Declaration unless:
  – the person remains at risk of further harm.
  – the matter is a serious one.

For our Review Activity we present a scenario from residential care. You should find the activity an easier one to complete than if we had set it in the person's own home.

Review Activity

This activity should take you about 20 minutes to complete.

Sheema Cupta is a 78-year-old woman who resides at The Elms, a privately run care home situated on the edge of the town centre.

Sheema was assessed under Section 47(1) of the *NHSCCA 1990*. It was felt that Sheema needed to be placed in a care home because:

- None of her relatives were able to offer her a home.

- Sheema was becoming forgetful, leaving gas taps on and was often found wandering the streets in a confused state.

- It was believed she couldn't cope at home, even with help.

Although Sheema is not mentally ill, she does have days when she is far from lucid in her thinking. You are Sheema's case manager and have just received an angry phone call from her daughter to say she has just been to The Elms and is deeply concerned that her mother is not being properly fed.

Write down the key issues here and what you think you should do in the light of the complaint.

Comment

Although some people may want to put pressure on you to turn this into a crisis, it isn't and hence it does not warrant immediate protection. There are already existing procedures to deal with such matters.

The key is to find out the facts by preparing a list of questions that need to be answered:

1. Is Sheema really being neglected?

2. Why is she not eating?

3. Is food offered appropriate to Sheema's cultural needs? (If not, there may be a case of abuse here through the home failing to recognise this).

4. Is Sheema currently mentally competent, i.e. does she have the capacity to make key decisions?

5. Is Sheema's daughter usually calm and self controlled herself?

6. Has The Elms taken positive steps to work through with Sheema why she needs to eat properly and look after herself.

The basis for your action should be to trigger a proper investigation by notifying the appropriate Adult Protection Manager and the CSCI office responsible for The Elms.

Information suggesting that abuse may have occurred within a Registered Care Home can come from any source. Whatever the source it is the responsibility of the relevant Registration and Inspection Unit to respond.

Emergency action is not warranted and Sheema should be consulted as to what action she wishes to be taken if it is proved that Sheema has been subject to any form of abuse such as lack of adequate food or failure of staff or others to notice rapid weight loss or lack of awareness of cultural need.

The referral to the Adult Protection Team will result in a Strategy Meeting being held to determine:

- what information needs to be obtained
- her capacity

before deciding what action can be taken.

It is expected the normal outcome from investigations will be one of the following:

1. A criminal offence has occurred and the police and Crown Prosecution Service will progress this.

2. Abuse has taken place, but at the request of the vulnerable adult (after multi-agency consideration) no prosecution will follow.

3. No criminal offence has been committed, but protection concerns remain.

4. The allegations are unsubstantiated and no further action needs to be taken.

We cannot tell you the outcome for Sheema as we do not yet know all the facts. Hence investigation and assessment should occur swiftly, but must always *precede* decision-making unless any vulnerable adult is at immediate risk of serious harm or any other form of abuse.

As we aim to equip you to be able to appraise situations of potential abuse or harm in people's own homes, it is important you are aware of the law relating to domestic violence, as in instances where the suspected abuse is *by a partner*; it is this route which should be followed.

Session Seven: The Law Relating to Domestic Violence

Upon completing this session you should be able to:

- Describe the dilemmas that confront professionals responding to domestic violence.

- Explain how the nature of privacy may affect my response to domestic violence.

- Describe legal provisions to protect victims of domestic violence and which enable them to remain in their own homes.

What is domestic violence?

Domestic violence is predominantly violence by men towards women in the family home. A very small number of men may be subject to domestic violence but this session is written to reflect the overwhelming majority of instances where men abuse women.

Domestic violence occurs within the bounds of private life and has therefore, until recently, not been fully acknowledged for what it is – criminal violence against women.

The nature of privacy

Activity 7.1

Consider for a moment the nature of privacy and what might be meant by 'private activities'. Can you draw a line that marks off your private life from other aspects of your life?

Comment

You probably regard some activities as quite clearly private. They go on within your home or household and concern nobody but those who live there. On the other hand there is an outside, public world where you carry out other legitimate activities.

Most of us strike a balance between public and private. However, this boundary is not rigidly defined. This can result in vigorous debate about civil liberties and about whether representatives of the public sphere may sometimes have a legitimate right to enter our private sphere, with or without our consent.

Activity 7.2

How could the issue of privacy relate to the woman seeking help because of violence in her household? This is an important issue, and we suggest you consider it for five to ten minutes and make notes before continuing.

Comment

The issue of privacy is relevant in a number of ways.

- Research suggests that women subject to violence in the home usually try to resolve the problem within the private sphere. Going public to seek help is a last resort and requires a significant degree of courage on their part. Social workers need to respect this.

- Some professional workers in public agencies including social workers, the police and health professionals have in the past given the impression that what goes on in private is up to those who live in that private space and nothing to do with the agencies – even when there is a degree of violence – unless extremely serious.

- As we saw above, a woman may opt to go to a solicitor for an injunction. This might be because she sees the problem as a private one that only she can resolve – a point that many social workers would take issue with.

- The possibility of public authorities intruding into private households, even when accepted as legitimate, is fraught with practical difficulties. Social workers who are concerned about their ability to intervene helpfully may be tempted not to take any action at all.

Criminal behaviour

Even though domestic violence may not always be recognised fully for what it is, it is important that you are aware that it constitutes criminal behaviour and that you acknowledge women's rights in the process. Both criminal and civil remedies are available. The police have powers of arrest (Section 25(3) *Police and Criminal Evidence Act 1984*) where there is a need to prevent injury or protect a child or a vulnerable person.

> *Under the Offences Against the Persons Act 1861 there are offences of common law assault, assault occasioning actual bodily harm, unlawful wounding and assault occasioning grievous bodily harm.*

(Braye and Preston-Shoot, 1997: 14)

Activity 7.3

Write down two or three reasons why women in situations of domestic violence are unlikely to benefit from the law as outlined above.

Comment

You may have thought about issues such as:

- Fear of being on ones own (without partner).

- Fear of retaliation.

- Feeling isolated and unsupported.

- Fear of turning to authority for help.

- Fear of being labelled as an inadequate parent if there are children in the home.

These are very real concerns and you should be able to make the connection here that all vulnerable adults abused in their own homes are likely to have similar feelings and thoughts.

Changing attitudes to domestic violence

Until recently the traditional picture was of a woman, after many attempts, leaving the home. She would then either be re-housed by the Housing Department as having 'priority need' (see the *Housing Act 1996*) or seek shelter in a women's refuge. Schedule 2, para 5 of the *Children Act 1989* states that where a person (here an abuser) proposes to move from the premises, the authority may assist that other person to obtain alternative accommodation. Assistance given may be cash. Although this measure still exists, today we hold the view that women who are subject to criminal violence in the home should remain in the home and the aggressor should be excluded. Powers did exist before to oust abusers, impose injunctions and attach the power of arrest, but somehow the system never seemed to work effectively to protect women.

There are two pieces of legislation specifically designed to tackle criminal violence in the home; the *Family Law Act 1996* and the *Protection from Harassment Act 1997*. We now describe the main powers contained within them.

The *Family Law Act 1996*: Occupation Orders

Sections 33–38 refer to Occupation Orders which deal with the occupation of the home and occupation rights. Such orders can require the respondent to leave the home, or part of it, not to come near the home, to allow the applicant to enter, or stay in the home, or part of it and can also decide what rights the respondent and applicant have to occupy the home. The terms of the order and the factors to be considered vary according to whether or not the applicant is entitled to occupy the property, and her relationship to the other party or parties.

An application for a Section 33 Order is made by persons who have a legal right to occupy:

- Spouses.

- Former spouses (with extended matrimonial rights).

- Cohabitants.

- Associated persons.

Section 35 Orders may be made where there is no existing right to occupy the property. Such an order, if made, cannot exceed six months but can be extended on more than one occasion for another period not to exceed 6 months.

Section 36 Orders refer to a cohabitant, or former cohabitant with no existing right to occupy the property. An order can be made up to six months and renewed on just one occasion.

Section 37 and 38 Orders can be made where neither party has the right to occupy a property. Section 37 deals with spouses and former spouses and Section 38 with cohabitants. The order deals with the respondent permitting the applicant to remain in a dwelling house or a part of it and excluding the respondent from defined areas of the dwelling.

Grounds for making Section 33, 35, 36, 37, and 38 Orders

In considering making any of these orders under the *Family Law Act 1996*, courts will take into account:

- The conduct of parties towards each other.

- Housing needs of both parties and any relevant child.

- Financial resources of the parties.

- The balance of harm test (to applicant and any child versus/respondent and any child).

- The existence of any current legal proceedings between the parties.

N.B. These proceedings apply only to dwellings that were occupied or intended to be occupied as the 'matrimonial' home.

Activity 7.4

Suggest two or three ways in which you think Occupation Orders help social workers to tackle domestic violence more appropriately.

Comment

The previous law was weak on enabling women escaping domestic violence to continue to live in their own homes. Occupation Orders directly address this issue. A further benefit you may have thought about is that Occupation Orders allow us to deal more directly with criminal violence in the home rather than looking to child protection as a potential solution. That said, the types of conditions which can be attached to an order and the enforcement powers are very similar to those under previous legislation. The reality remains that these measures may not be very effective against a determined man who wishes to cause violence or grief to the woman.

Non-molestation orders

Molestation is now legally defined in the *Family Law Act 1996*, Section 42 as:

- Threat of physical or sexual violence.

- Carrying out physical or sexual violence.

- Phone calls.

- Letters.

Non-molestation is related to the conduct and behaviour of the molester. An order can be brought against specific or general acts of molestation and made for a specific period or until further notice. The court may attach the power of arrest to an order which allows the police to make an arrest without the need of a warrant.

Until recently a breach of a non-molestation Order was dealt with as contempt of court. Although this remains an option, the law has now been tightened up and under Section 42A(1) of the *Domestic Violence, Crime and Victims Act 2004* it is now:

an offence for a person without excuse to do anything that he is prohibited from doing by a non-molestation order.

A person guilty of an offence, under Section 42A(5) is liable on conviction or indictment to up to five years imprisonment, a fine or both, and on summary conviction, up to 12 months imprisonment, a fine or both.

Activity 7.5

When do you believe you will need to seek a Non-molestation Order rather than an Occupation Order?

Comment

Whenever an Occupation Order is made you should give consideration to the appropriateness of a Non-molestation Order. People who use criminal violence in the home tend to be both persistent and intimidating. The Non-molestation Order is designed to prevent retaliation and reduce the fear people in violent situations have about complaining or about taking action.

Section 45 Ex Parte Orders

The court has the power to make an initial Occupation Order or initial Non-molestation Order on an ex parte basis. The court must consider:

- Risk of significant harm to the applicant or a relevant child, attributable to the conduct of the respondent, if the order is not made immediately.

- Whether it is likely the applicant will be deterred or prevented from pursuing the application if an order is not made immediately.

Section 46 Undertakings

Where a court has the power to make an Occupation Order or a Non-molestation Order it can accept an undertaking:

- Section 46 (2) power of arrest cannot be attached to an undertaking.

- Section 46 (3) the court must not accept an undertaking where a power of arrest would be more appropriate.

- Section 46 (4) if the undertaking is breached it can be enforced as if it were an order of the court.

The *Protection from Harassment Act 1997*

Under Section 1(1) A person must not pursue a course of conduct which amounts to harassment of another and which they know or ought to know, amounts to the harassment of the other.

Under Section 4(1) a person whose course of conduct causes another to fear, on at least two occasions, that violence will be used against him/her, is guilty of an offence if he/she knows or ought to know that his/her conduct will cause the other so to fear on each of those occasions.

Police officers can arrest without warrant and the offence carries a maximum punishment of five years imprisonment.

Courts may also impose restraining orders on those convicted which also carry, if breached, a maximum punishment of five years imprisonment.

Activity 7.6

The *Family Law Act 1996* and the *Protection from Harassment Act 1997* should help to enable women to live in their own homes and aggressors to be excluded. However, suggest one or two problems which might emerge in practice.

Comment

You may have thought about women needing to be aware that the law has been strengthened in their favour. We have already mentioned Women's Aid, which runs phone line support, but it is important that social workers work collaboratively with them to get the message of zero tolerance across as widely as possible. You may also have thought that the attitude adopted by the police is particularly important in these situations.

To whom the legislation applies

The previous *Family Law Act 1996* applied almost exclusively to married couples but the *Domestic Violence, Crime and Victims Act 2004* broadens the range of situations in which it can be applied.

Section 41 of the *Family Law Act 1996* required a court to:

> *Consider the nature of the relationships of cohabitants, or former cohabitants with regard to their non-married status.*

This section is *repealed*.

Section 36(6)(e) of the *FLA 1996*, when the court is giving consideration whether to give the right to occupy to a cohabitant, or former cohabitant with no existing right, the *DVCVA 2004* now requires courts to give consideration to the 'level of commitment' involved in the relationship.

The *DVCVA 2004* extends the definition to same sex couples by removing 'cohabitants' from Section 62(1)(a) *FLA 1996* and substituting:

> *. . . two persons who, although not married to each other, are living together as husband and wife or (if of same sex) in an equivalent relationship.*

Police powers

The *Police and Criminal Evidence Act 1984* empowers the police under Section 17 (1)(b) to enter and search premises without a warrant for the purposes of saving life and limb or preventing serious damage to property. Under Section 17(1)(b) the police are given the same power of entry to arrest for an arrestable offence. Section 25 allows the police to arrest without warrant on a number of grounds, including that the constable has reasonable grounds for believing that arrest is necessary to prevent the person from causing physical injury to themselves or others, or causing loss or damage to property.

PACE has a power (Section 80) to compel a spouse or partner to attend court for the purpose of giving evidence. It is infrequently used, but addressed the problem perceived by police of victims' complaints being withdrawn. It also overturns years of common law stating that a husband and wife could not be compelled to give evidence against each other.

Review Activity

This activity should take you about 15 minutes to complete.

Under what circumstances do you believe domestic violence legislation should be used if there is a concern about abuse between two partners. Write down two or three.

Comment

The domestic violence legislation you have learnt about in this session can only be used if the abuse takes place within marriage, or by someone living with another as husband and wife or in an equivalent relationship if a same sex couple.

Domestic violence legislation is only used where a person has capacity as they will need to seek a civil order against their partner. It cannot be used where the person lacks capacity.

Domestic violence will become a safeguarding matter if the victim:

- lacks capacity
- is a vulnerable adult
- is dependent on their partner for their care.

The next session will help you address issues of capacity as this is a pivotal concept in safeguarding.

Session Eight: Considering Capacity

Session objectives

Upon completing this session you should be able to:

- Outline the principles which apply when determining capacity and describe the practical test used to determine capacity.

- Explain the new provisions contained in the *Mental Capacity Act 2005*.

- Describe the dilemmas posed by capacity and compulsion.

Introduction

As you will have seen throughout this workbook:

- Capacity is a key concern in safeguarding especially when considering abuse within a person's own home.

- Essentially the decision as to whether or not to intervene against the wishes of the victim or potential victim, will depend upon whether or not it is believed the vulnerable person has capacity.

Let's begin by looking at a clear case where you should *not* intervene.

A GP telephones to express concerns about an 88-year-old man living in a bungalow on his own.

He believes the man is at risk because:

- He could become ill at any time.

- He may be unable to look after himself.

- He may be at risk by having his bungalow broken into and thereby at risk from physical injury from intruders.

This case obviously warrants a proper risk assessment but is *not* a safeguarding issue.

An experienced social worker visited and it transpired the man was:

- A war veteran.

- In general good physical health for his age.

- Mentally competent.

He explained how he fought for freedom in the War and claims the right to live and die in his own home. He points out that he will contact any relevant party should he believe he needs assistance.

The social worker respects his wishes, informs the GP of his decision and writes up the visit on file.

Activity 8.1

This activity should take you about 15 minutes to complete.

Two weeks later the man is found dead at home. He has been there for three or four days. The GP is furious and contacts the local television station, claiming Social Care have been derelict in their duties.

Write down what you believe to be the issues here.

Comment

In this hypothetical, but possibly true, example, the Director contacted the local Social Care office, went and read the file and spoke with the social worker. The Director offered the social worker support and reassurance and then went to visit the man's relatives.

On television that evening the Director asked the GP if he had obtained the relatives' permission to discuss the case publically – he had not.

So issue one is about confidentiality.

The Director then added there would be no investigation as the social worker had acted appropriately.

Issue two is about support for the worker.

Social Care had simply respected the person's wishes to live and die in their own home.

So, the third issue is about respecting the wishes of people who *have* capacity. Hence:

- All cases must be dealt with confidentially.
- We need to support people throughout the investigative process.
- We must respect vulnerable adults wishes so long as they are mentally capable of making a decision.

Safeguarding Vulnerable Adults. © 2008 Denis A. Hart. www.russellhouse.co.uk

Unwise decisions

One of the biggest dilemmas you are likely to face in your practice is whether a vulnerable person's decision is:

irrational (a sign they may lack capacity) or simply 'unwise'.

Spend a few moments and think of when you last made an unwise decision. Many people refer to speeding, or jumping a red traffic light, but some explain they saw a multi-coloured garment in a shop window, paid £100 for it and when they got it home and tried it on thought, I can't wear this. Part of being human is that we are free to make unwise decisions, even decisions other people don't approve of. How often has someone been told, uninvited, 'you shouldn't have married him or her!'

So when does an unwise decision become so irrational it suggests a lack of capacity?

Activity 8.2

This activity should take you about 15 minutes to complete.

When you call on Mavis you notice that her flat is unclean, there are piles of dirty laundry, and she appears thin and nervous. Mavis, however, is adamant that while she gives her son £200 per week, he is not abusing her and she is doing so because he provides her with care.

Write down the dilemmas this presents for you.

Comment

Mavis is free to do whatever she likes with her money so long as she has capacity.

Mavis, however, seems to be being neglected in spite of paying her son £200 per week as:

- The flat isn't being properly cleaned.
- The laundry isn't being done.

and

- Mavis *may* be thin through not eating enough or not eating enough of the right food.

Until recently you have had a dilemma here for, as long as she *has* capacity, you have not been able to do anything against her wishes.

However, that doesn't mean you should leave things there. Remember *No Secrets* and being aware of the need to follow local Adult Protection Procedures. Although adult protection may confirm capacity and feel there is no need for any legal intervention, you could still feel it is wise to attempt to persuade Mavis to have an assessment carried out of her needs. This might let you eventually get into the thorny debate as to whether or not her son gives 'best value' care and it gives you a possible lever whereby you can remain involved without offending the *Human Rights Act 1998*.

The right to respect of privacy in family life is being re-interpreted as it is now recognised that no-one living in a family home should suffer harm or abuse and that this right should not be interpreted in such a way that it allows harm or abuse to continue. Indeed, under the *MCA, 2005*, Section 44 makes wilful neglect a *criminal* matter.

However, at present, Mavis's decision is simply unwise but *not* irrational. We can try to help, support and persuade but should not infringe upon her Rights.

Principles underlying the *Mental Capacity Act 2005*

Section 1 of the Act lays down a number of key principles:

1.   A person must be assumed to have capacity unless it is established that he lacks capacity.

2.   A person is not to be treated as unable to make a decision unless all practicable steps to help him to do so have been taken without success.

3.   A person is not to be treated as unable to make a decision merely because he makes an unwise decision.

4.   An act done, or decision made, under this Act for, or on behalf of a person who lacks capacity must be done, or made, *in his best interests*.

5.   Before the act is done, or the decision is made, regard must be had to whether the purpose for which it is needed can be as effectively achieved in a way that is less restrictive of the person's rights and freedom of action.

Activity 8.3

This activity should take you about 15 minutes to complete.

In the light of these principles return to the case of Mavis Brown. When you visited her, did you consider these principles in determining her decision was simply 'unwise'?

Apply them now, one by one and write down your responses.

Comment

With reference to the list above, the following points apply:

1. Always assume a person has capacity unless matters arise which bring this into doubt.

2. Mavis may have been tired when you visited, even a little confused, but did you take the time to express your concerns?

3. Mavis probably said she would rather pay someone she knows to keep her company than go into a home. She knows her son is taking advantage, but thinks it's a better option. You may not agree – you may think she's 'unwise' but her argument is actually quite rational.

4. Doesn't apply here as Mavis *has* capacity but if she didn't then whatever action you decided to take against her wishes *must* be in her best interests.

5. The least restrictive option available.

Determining capacity

The Act does not address incapacity globally but rather capacity is to be dealt with on:

an issue by issue basis.

Under Section 2, a person lacks capacity in relation to a matter if:

. . . at the material time he is unable to make a decision for himself in relation to a matter because of an impairment of, or disturbance of mind, whether permanent or temporary.

For us, Section 3 is of greatest significance because it provides a *practical* test we should use to:

determine capacity to make a specific *decision.*

Activity 8.4

This activity should take you about 10 minutes to complete.

Write down what you believe are the key issues to consider in determining capacity.

Comment

You probably thought about questions such as these:

*   Do they appear to be able to absorb the information?

*   Can they process it?

*   Do they appear to be able to reach a reasoned conclusion?

The actual 'capacity test' which has been devised is quite similar to these thoughts. The 'capacity test' itself is made up of four elements:

1. Can the person *absorb* relevant information?

2. Can they retain it long enough to process it?

3. Can they weigh up the pros and cons of each option and reach a conclusion?

4. Can they communicate their decision to others?

If the answer to all four questions is 'yes', their decision is inviolate. If not, they may be considered incapacitated with regard to making that particular decision.

Section 3 of the *MCA 2005* specifies that a person is unable to make a decision for himself if he is unable:

(a) To understand the information relevant to the decision.

(b) To retain that information.

(c) To use or weigh that information as part of the process of making the decision.

or

(d) To communicate his decision (whether by talking, using sign language or any other means).

If it is determined the person lacks capacity to make the specific decision in question then those acting on his behalf must act in his best interests and take into account:

• How long the person may continue to lack capacity.

• Past and present wishes and feelings.

• The beliefs and values which would have influenced his decision.

and consult with:

• Anyone named by the person.

• Anyone caring for the person or interested in their welfare.

• Any donee of a lasting power of attorney granted by the person.

• Any deputy appointed for the person by the court.

A new criminal offence

The *Mental Capacity Act 2005*, which came into effect in October 2007, creates a new *criminal* offence of ill treatment or wilful neglect of a vulnerable adult who lacks capacity.

Section 44 states that if someone cares for someone who lacks capacity or where it is reasonable for them to believe they lack capacity, and they ill treat or wilfully neglect the person they are caring for under Section 44(2), they are guilty of an offence and, under Section 44(3), liable:

(a) *on summary conviction to imprisonment for a term not exceeding 12 months or a fine not exceeding the statutory maximum, or both.*

(b) *on conviction on indictment, to imprisonment for a term not exceeding 5 years or a fine or both.*

Activity 8.5

This activity should take you about 10 minutes to complete.

Re-read the scenario of Mavis Brown, the 81-year-old who gives her son £200 per week to look after her but still appears to be neglected.

Social Care is considering removing Mavis from her home, believing she lacks the capacity to make a meaningful decision about the care she needs and that by so doing it opens up the possibility that her son can be charged under Section 44 with willful neglect.

What are the key issues here?

Comment

I think it's a case of hang on a minute. One problem with new legislation is that some people will rush to use it without considering the broader picture:

> remember the legal dilemma damned if you do, damned if you don't.

Mavis' lot is not a happy one at present but she may well feel 'better the devil you know'. You may be frustrated, even annoyed, that the son is getting paid for doing nothing and is at best taking advantage of his mother, but:

> . . . this doesn't give us the right to take away Mavis' right to make her own decision.

Before doing anything we need to be certain that Mavis really *isn't* able to grasp and retain the information we provided her with about her son's behaviour and we equally need to be certain that any decisions made, or actions taken, are:

> in her 'best interests'.

There seems little doubt Mavis is to some degree:

Safeguarding Vulnerable Adults. © 2008 Denis A. Hart. www.russellhouse.co.uk

- Being financially abused.

and

- Being neglected.

But we also need to consider where Mavis will live if:

- It is believed she is unable to care for herself.

- Her son is the only possible full-time carer.

Apart from the son potentially being charged under Section 44 of the *Mental Capacity Act 2005* you also need to be aware that the *Domestic Violence, Crime and Victims Act 2004* introduces an offence under Section 5 of:

Causing or allowing the death of a child or vulnerable adult, whereby:

A person is guilty of an offence if:

(a) *a child or vulnerable adult dies as a result of the unlawful act of a person who:*
    (i) *was a member of the same household and*
    (ii) *had frequent contact with him*

(b) *that the person was such at the time of that act*

(c) *at that time there was a significant risk of serious physical harm being caused by the unlawful act of such a person.*

Moreover, it becomes an offence if they:

. . . failed to take such steps as could reasonably have been taken to protect from the risk and the act occurred in circumstances of the kind they could foresaw or ought to have foreseen.

The new legislation requires us to weigh up everything including all the possible outcomes. Remember:

- *On the one hand* you could be accused of breaching the Right to Respect Privacy in Family Life if you intervene against the wishes of a person with capacity.

- *On the other hand* you could be sued if you failed to adequately protect a person who lacks capacity by seeking an Order of Declaratory Relief.

You will now appreciate how crucial it is to be clear about when people are, and are not, capable.

Section 42 of the *MCA 2005* requires the Lord Chancellor to produce Codes of Practice, one of which will be *for the guidance of persons assessing whether a person has capacity in relation to any matter* and another *for the guidance of persons acting in connection with the care or treatment of another person.*

Capacity and compulsion

The problem with applying the notion of lack of capacity, or incapacity, to practice is that it:

> *takes away rights of individuals.*

One of the most notorious examples is that of:

> *the compulsory removal of older people from their own homes under Section 47 of the National Assistance Act 1948.*

A community physician may apply for an initial order for up to three months if the person is:

- Suffering from grave chronic disease. Aged, infirm or physically incapacitated.
- Living in unsanitary conditions.

and

- Unable to care for themselves.
- Not receiving proper care and attention from other persons.

The *Human Rights Act 1998*

The *Human Rights Act 1998* sees the United Kingdom adopting the Articles of the European Convention and requires that:

> *all legislation past, present and future, be consistent with the Articles of the European Convention.*

Of relevance here are Articles 5, 6 and 8:

- Article 5 – The Right to liberty and security.
- Article 6 – The Right to a fair trail.
- Article 8 – The Right to the respect of privacy in family life.

However, you should note that all three of these Articles are conditional rather than absolute.

Activity 8.6

This activity should take you about 15 minutes to complete.

Mrs Khan is a 78-year-old who lives alone. Neighbours have complained about the stench of rotting food coming from her house and the way she discards rubbish into her garden, attracting rats. Social Care has decided to seek an Order for her to be compulsorily removed under Section 47, *NAA 1948* claiming she poses a risk to the health of others.

Write down whether you believe the proposed action is consistent with the *Human Rights Act 1998*.

Comment

There is no breach of Article 8 as the Right to respect in family life can be specifically over-ridden if someone poses a risk to public health. Likewise there is no breach of Article 5 as the Right to liberty can be over-ridden and allows for the:

> *. . . lawful detention of persons for the prevention of infectious diseases, persons of unsound mind, alcoholics, drug addicts or vagrants.*

Although older people can appeal to the Crown Court under Section 47 of the *National Assistance Act 1948*, compulsory removal is a decision of the court whereby there is:

- No obligation for the person to be informed of their Rights.

- No obligation for them to be legally represented.

and

- Legal aid is not available.

Thus, we believe Section 47 breaches Article 6 of the Convention whereby:

> *Everyone who is deprived of his liberty by arrest or detention should be entitled to take proceedings by which the lawfulness of his detention shall be decided speedily by a court and his release ordered if the detention is unlawful.*

In 1948 there was no separate Mental Health legislation and we believe the origins of this Section were embedded in the notion that older people only live in such conditions because they are mentally ill or lack capacity and therefore they wouldn't be able to understand the legal proceedings. Our argument is that in order to deliver natural justice the Mental Health Act should be the *only* legislation used for compulsory removal as there is:

> *an automatic right of appeal to the Mental Health Review Tribunal and legal aid is provided.*

In recent years society has increasingly gone down the road of compulsion, so we must welcome the creation of Independent mental capacity advocates under Section 35 of the *Mental Capacity Act 2005*.

Section 35(1) stipulates that:

> *The appropriate authority must make such arrangements as it considers reasonable to enable persons (independent mental capacity advocates) to be available to represent and support persons.*

Independent mental capacity advocates are created to give *specific* support with regards to the:

- Provision of serious medical treatment by an NHS body (Section 7).

- Provision of accommodation by an NHS body (Section 38).

- Provision of accommodation by local authority (Section 39).

Essentially the 'advocate' will check out that what is being proposed on behalf of the person who lacks capacity:

> *is indeed **in their best interests***.

Although the *Mental Health Act 2007* amends the *Mental Capacity Act 2005* by introducing new safeguards when seeking to deprive people who lack capacity of their liberty, amazingly Schedule 9 *exempts* 547, *NAA 1948* from the new procedures as 'no complaint has been made to the European Court'.

A further element of compulsion is found in Civil Orders of Declaratory Relief.

Declaratory relief

A Common Law Order of Declaratory Relief originated in the 14th century but recently lawyers have pushed local authorities to apply for it whenever they believe a vulnerable adult:

- Is likely to experience harm or abuse.

and

- Lacks capacity.

Such lawyers have further argued that a vulnerable adult who lacks capacity and subsequently experiences harm or abuse may later be:

> *entitled to damages if the local authority failed to seek a Declaration on the grounds the harm or injury suffered 'could have been avoided'.*

This pressure has added to the shift that whereas a few years back adult protection was more likely to be criticised for failing to do, it is now more likely to be legally challenged for:

failing not to do.

Summary

In this Session we have introduced you to the key principles of the *Mental Capacity Act 2005*. We now offer you a Review Activity to check your understanding.

Review Activity

This activity should take you about 15 minutes to complete.

A neighbour calls you over whilst you are visiting another service user. He explains that Albert Brown, who lives opposite, is covered in bruises and is regularly assaulted by his nephew.

Write down what you have learnt from this session to help you progress the neighbour's 'referral'.

Comment

1. The first question is, is this actually a 'referral'? The issue needs to be formalised.

2. Is Albert Brown a vulnerable adult?

3. Has Albert capacity? This will be determined by applying the practical test found in Section 3.

4. Do I have *reasonable cause* to believe a crime has been committed.

5. Act in a person's best interests, be sure not to jump to conclusions, keep your practice balanced.

In this case Albert's bruising was caused by his blood-thinning medication. The neighbour was trying to get the nephew locked up as he was next in line to inherit Albert's estate. The moral of the tale here is:

don't go on a mission to blindly protect.

Scenarios are *never* as straightforward as they seem. Take time to reflect first – which is why we refer to Safeguarding. Remember, it is difficult to undo something we shouldn't have done, or assumed, which is why we must never over-react. The key is to:

always ensure we adopt a balanced approach.

To help you further we now present a paradigm we have devised which we believe clarifies your duties, responsibilities and powers.

1. Whenever possible work in *partnership* with the vulnerable adult and their carer(s), *but*

2. if you become concerned about the *welfare* of any vulnerable adult, *and*

3. the carer will not co-operate with you, *then*

4. place the welfare of the vulnerable adult as your paramount responsibility, *unless*

5. they *have* the capacity to make the specific decision being asked of them.

Session Nine: Protecting People Who Lack Capacity

Session objectives

Upon completing this session you should be able to:

- Describe the main provisions of the *Mental Capacity Act 2005*.

- Explain how finances are protected.

- Explain how healthcare and treatment issues are dealt with for people who lack capacity.

- Describe what is meant by an advance decision and explain how, and when, these should be used.

Introduction

The *Mental Capacity Act 2005* provides,

> . . . the legal framework for acting and making decisions on behalf of individuals who lack the mental capacity to make particular decisions for themselves.

(Code of Practice to the MCA 2005, TSO, 2007: 15)

So far in this workbook we have assumed the person *has* capacity; now we move on to look at those who are unable to make a specific decision.

The decisions that can be taken on behalf of vulnerable people who lack capacity come under two broad headings:

1. Financial affairs.

2. Affairs related to personal care needs.

Financial affairs

We are going to start you off by thinking about someone's right to give away money!

Activity 9.1

This activity should take you about 15 minutes to complete.

Marion Smith is a 76-year-old. She has been found in the local shopping centre giving away £20 notes to passers-by.

Write down your views.

Comment

In principle it is fine for Marion to 'redistribute her wealth'. We are all allowed to dispose of our assets as we choose and the more cynical might have responded 'I wish I'd been there'.

In practice the key issue is 'Does Marion *really* mean to give away her money' (i.e. is that what she *intends*). Indeed, it is the concept of intention which helps us to determine capacity in these circumstances as well as when dealing with criminal matters.

Until recently the legal aspects were dealt with by Sections 93-98 of the *Mental Health Act 1983* and the *Enduring Powers of Attorney Act 1985*.

These have both been *repealed* with the advent of the *Mental Capacity Act 2005* effective from October, 2007

Under Section 9 (1) a person who currently has capacity, but is likely to lose capacity permanently or temporarily in the foreseeable future, may have another person legally appointed to make decisions on their behalf once capacity has been lost.

A Lasting Power of Attorney is one whereby 'the donor confers on the donee(s) authority to make decisions about:

(a) Their personal welfare or specified matters concerning their personal welfare.

and

(b) Their property and affairs or specific matters concerning their property and affairs.'

The donee(s) must act in the 'best interests' of the donor.

A person wishing to draw up such a power, or have one created by a friend or relative should:

> *always take legal advice from a solicitor.*

The powers conferred on the donee(s) to deal with property and affairs are specified under Section 18 (1):

- The control and management of their property.

- The sale, exchange, charging, gift or other disposition of their property.

- The acquisition of property on their behalf.

- The carrying on of their profession, trade or business.

- The taking of a decision which will have the effect of dissolving a partnership of which the donor is a member.

- The carrying out of any contract on their behalf.

- The discharge of their debts or obligations whether legally enforceable or not.

- The settlement of any property whether for the benefit of the donor or for the benefit of others.

- The execution of a will.

- The exercise of any power vested in the donor whether beneficially or as trustee or otherwise.

- The conduct of legal proceedings in the donor's name or on their behalf.

These aspects are shown in a more practical form in para 7.36 of the Code of Practice, p125.

The donor can choose one person or several to make different kinds of decisions.

Any previous powers given under the former *Enduring Powers of Attorney Act 1985*:

> *remain valid for 30 years.*

The Lasting Power of Attorney must be registered with the:

> *Office of the Public Guardian before it can be used and as soon after the donor makes it as possible.*

Remember the donor *must* have capacity at the time the LPA is drawn up.

Activity 9.2

This activity should take you about 15 minutes to complete.

Write down two or three things a donee should consider when acting in the best interest of the donor who conferred the power on them.

Comment

Basically the donee should consider:

the donor's past and present wishes and feelings, beliefs and values.

And should consult:

- Anyone involved in caring for the donor.

- Close relatives and anyone else with an interest in the donor's welfare.

- Other attorneys appointed by the donor.

Restraint

Section 11 of the *MCA 2005* prevents the donee(s) from doing anything to *restrain* the donor unless:

- The donee believes the donor lacks capacity with regard to the matter in question.

and

- The donee reasonably believes it is necessary to do the act to prevent harm to the donor.

and

- The act is a proportionate response to:

  (a) The likelihood of the donor suffering harm, and

  (b) The seriousness of that harm.

Remember even once a Lasting Power of Attorney has been made, the Court of Protection still has powers over the LPA.

Activity 9.3

This activity should take you about 15 minutes to complete.

Write down an example where the Court of Protection may exercise powers over the LPA?

Comment

An obvious example would be when a person with a power began to dispose of the donors assets to organised extreme Right-wing parties when their own political beliefs had been middle of the road to non-committal.

Here the donee clearly is not acting in the best interests of that person and the court can:

> *remove an attorney in such circumstances.*

The Court of Protection also has powers to:

- Determine whether an LPA is valid.

and

- Give directions about the way the LPA is used.

The Court of Protection

Going back to Marion who is continuing to give £20 notes away. If it is believed that she *already* lacks capacity an LPA *cannot* be made.

It is now down to an interested party to apply to the Court of Protection under Section 50:

Section 50(3) specifies:

'In deciding whether to grant permission the court must have regard to:

(a) The applicants' connection with the person to whom the application relates.

(b) The reasons for the application.

(c) The benefit to the person to whom the application relates of a proposed order or directions.

and

(d) Whether the benefit can be achieved in any other way'.

N.B. There is a right of appeal against any decision to the Court of Appeal.

The Code of Practice specifies that the Court of Protection may:

> *. . . make declarations, decisions and orders on financial and welfare matters affecting people who lack, or alleged to lack, capacity.*

> *Appoint deputies to make decisions for those who lack capacity to make those decisions.*
> (para 8.13, Code of Practice, 2007: 141)

Appointees

Sometimes someone can be appointed under Social Security Regulations to claim and collect benefits or pensions on behalf of a person who lacks capacity to manage their own benefits. The appointee is permitted to use the money claimed to meet the person's needs. The DWP appoints trustworthy people and is also responsible for removing people from that role if concerns arise.

Inappropriate behaviour

The Code of Practice under para 8.13 reminds us that the Court of Protection also has the power to:

remove deputies or attorneys who act inappropriately.

The *Fraud Act 2006* creates a new offence of:

fraud by abuse of position.

This offence may apply to:

- Attorneys under a Lasting Power of Attorney (LPA) or an Enduring Power of Attorney (EPA),

or

- Deputies appointed by the Court of Protection to make financial decisions on behalf of a person who lacks capacity.

The Code of Practice adds:

Attorneys and deputies may be guilty of fraud if they dishonestly abuse their position, intend to benefit themselves or others, and cause loss or expose a person to the risk of loss. People who suspect fraud should report the case to the police.

(op cit, para 14.7: 247)

Health and personal care

The previous *Enduring Power of Attorney Act 1985* only gave those with powers (EPA), or the Court of Protection powers, to address a vulnerable adult's finances. What is significant about the *Mental Capacity Act 2005* is it extends those powers to decisions about health and personal care, including advance decisions.

Section 5 of the Act allows carers, healthcare and social care staff to carry out certain tasks without fear of liability when the person lacks capacity to consent to them. People providing care of this sort do not therefore need to obtain formal authority to act.

Section 5(1) provides possible protection so long as the action taken is in that person's best interests.

Activity 9.4

This activity should take you about 15 minutes to complete.

Write down four or five examples of personal or health care where you believe you can act on behalf of a person who lacks capacity without incurring liability.

Comment

The actual list is detailed under para 6.5 of the Code of Practice, p95.

Personal care

- Helping with:
  - Washing, dressing or personal hygiene
  - Eating and drinking
  - Communication
  - Mobility (moved around)
  - Taking part in education, social or leisure activities

- Going into a person's home to drop off shopping or to see if they are all right.

- Doing shopping or buying goods with the person's money.

- Arranging household services (repairs or maintenance).

- Providing services that help around the home.

- Undertaking actions related to community care services such as arranging day care, residential accommodation or nursing care.

- Helping someone to move home.

Healthcare and treatment

- Carrying out diagnostic examinations and tests.

- Providing professional medical, dental and similar treatment.

- Giving medication.

- Taking someone to hospital for assessment or treatment.

- Providing nursing care.

- Carrying out any necessary medical procedures or therapies.

- Providing care in an emergency.

In some cases a person who lacks capacity to make a significant decision may need representation and support from:

an Independent Mental Capacity Advocate (IMCA).

This is dealt with under Sections 35 and 36 of the *MCA 2005*.

Section 35 requires local authorities to make arrangements to enable vulnerable adults to receive representation and support with regards to:

- Serious medical treatment by the NHS (Section 37).

- Provision of accommodation by the NHS body (Section 38).

and

- Provision of accommodation by the local authority (Section 39).

IMCAs may take copies of:

- Any health record.

- Any social services records.

- Any records held by a person registered under Part 2 which they consider relevant.

Section 36

This is designed so the IMCA can help the vulnerable adult understand the nature and scope of the decision that needs to be made. It spells out the functions of IMCAs namely to:

- Providing support so the person can participate as fully as possible in decision making.

- Providing and evaluating relevant information.

- Ascertaining what the persons wishes and feelings might be if they had capacity based on their beliefs and values.

- Exploring the options available.

- Obtaining a further medical opinion when treatment is proposed and the advocate believes this necessary.

The IMCA will also be able to challenge, or provide assistance for challenging any relevant decision.

Activity 9.5

This activity should take you about 15 minutes to complete.

Write down how we could *prevent* the need for an IMCA to be appointed.

Comment

In the same way LPAs allow people with capacity to appoint attorney(s) to make decisions on their behalf once they have lost the capacity, the *MCA 2005* creates a new measure, that of being able to make:

advance decisions.

Advance decisions

Dealt with by Sections 24–26 an advance decision allows a person with capacity, aged 18 or over to specify that at a later time when capacity has been lost:

. . . specified treatment is not to be carried out or continued.

(Section 24(1))

The person may later alter, or withdraw, that advance decision as long as they still have capacity.

The advance decision is *not* valid if the person later creates a LPA giving the donee(s) powers to give or refuse consent to treatment (Section 25(2)(b)). Nor is it valid if:

. . . circumstances exist which the vulnerable adult did not anticipate at the time of the advance decision and which would have affected his decision had he anticipated them.

(Section 25 (4)(c))

Advance decisions must be made in writing and signed by the vulnerable adult or under direction by another person in their presence.

In a life-threatening situation someone giving treatment may go against an advance decision to withhold treatment whilst seeking a decision as to whether the advance decision from the Court should hold.

Under Section 26(4) the court may declare an advance decision:

(a)   Exists.

(b)   Is valid.

(c)   Is applicable to treatment.

Where a person lacks capacity the court may appoint a Deputy to make any relevant decision on behalf of the vulnerable adult whether about personal care, health care or their financial affairs. (Sections 15–21 apply.)

The Bournewood Judgement and the deprivation of liberty

The Bournewood case concerned an autistic man with severe learning disabilities who was informally admitted to Bournewood Hospital under common law. The European Court of Human Rights found he had been unlawfully deprived of his liberty due to the lack of safeguards and speedy access to a court.

The *Mental Health Act 2007* amends the *Mental Capacity Act 2005* and thereby introduces:

> *new deprivation of liberty safeguards.*

The Safeguards apply to those aged 18 or over who:

- Suffer from a disorder or disability of the mind.

and

- Lack the capacity to give consent to the arrangements made for their care or treatment.

and

- For whom such care is considered, after an independent assessment to be a necessary, and proportionate, response in their best interests, to protect them from harm.

The procedure cannot be used to detain people in hospital for treatment of mental disorder when the *Mental Health Act 1983* could be used instead.

The *Mental Capacity Act 2005*, from April 2009, will not permit someone to be deprived of liberty without an *authorisation*, unless this is a personal welfare decision made by the Court of Protection. Whenever a hospital or care home identifies that a person who lacks capacity is being, or risks being, deprived of their liberty, they *must* apply to the 'supervisory body' for authorisation. Where a person is in a care home, the supervisory body will be the relevant local authority. Where the person is in a care home, the supervisory body will be the relevant local authority. Where the person is in a hospital, this will be the relevant Primary Care Trust.

Authorisation should be obtained in advance except in urgent circumstances when the hospital or care home may issue an urgent authorisation, with written reasons, pending a standard authorisation.

Anyone concerned, e.g. a family member, can apply to the supervisory body to trigger an assessment.

When a supervisory body receives a request for authorisation of deprivation of liberty they must obtain six assessments in keeping with those laid down in the *Mental Health Act 2007*:

1. **Age assessment** – they are aged 18 or over.

2. **Mental health assessment** – they are suffering from a mental disorder.

3. **Mental capacity assessment** – they lack capacity to decide whether to be admitted to, or remain in, the hospital or care home.

4. **Eligibility assessment** – they are eligible if detained under the *MHA 1983* subject to a requirement under the *MHA 1983* that conflicts with the authorisation, e.g. a guardianship order, subject to powers of recall under the *MHA 1983, or* unless the application is to enable mental health treatment in hospital and they object to being in hospital or to the treatment in question.

5. **Best interests assessment** – the proposed course of action constitutes a deprivation of liberty and is:
   – in the best interests of the person to be subject to authorisation, *and*
   – necessary to prevent harm, *and*
   – a proportionate response to the likelihood of suffering harm and the seriousness of that harm.

6. **No refusals assessment** – the authorisation sought does not conflict with a valid decision by a donee of a lasting power of attorney, or by a deputy appointed for the person by the Court of Protection, and is not for the purpose of giving treatment that would conflict with a valid and applicable advance decision made by the person.

N.B. Best Interests and mental health assessments must be carried out by different assessors.

The best interest assessor must take account of the views of anyone named by the person, anyone involved in their care or concerned with their welfare, any attorney and any deputy. The best interests assessor may:

> *recommend conditions to be attached to any authorisation such as contact with family members.*

Where a person has no relevant family an Independent Mental Capacity Advocate (IMCA) should be appointed.

The maximum period for authorisation will be 12 months.

For a detailed discussion you should consult the DoH *Mental Capacity Act 2005: Deprivation of Liberty Safeguards* and the Code of Practice on the Deprivation of Liberty Safeguards which is to be added to the current Code of Practice to the *Mental Capacity Act 2005*.

Review Activity

This activity should take you about 20 minutes to complete.

A person has been diagnosed with HIV and has a low T cell count and high viral load. This means they could become very ill, or even die, quite quickly and suddenly.

They tell you they don't want to be given repeated doses of Septrin (a powerful anti-biotic) if they repeatedly develop AIDs-related pneumonia.

Write down what you believe can be done to:

- Respect their wishes.

and

- Address their best interests.

Comment

The crucial matter here is do they have the capacity to decide they wouldn't wish to be kept alive using Septrin. So we begin by applying the capacity test in Section 3.

If they *have* capacity they could:

- Sign an advance decision.
- Draw up a LPA for someone to make future decisions on their behalf with regards to their health care.

The person may be traumatised at present and in emotional turmoil so we need to catch them at a more lucid moment. However, it is equally possible they will rapidly deteriorate.

Ideally, we need to catch them at the peak of lucidity and then suggest they take one of the two options above. However, their request is so *specific* that it would appear that they *are* making this decision with a sound mind.

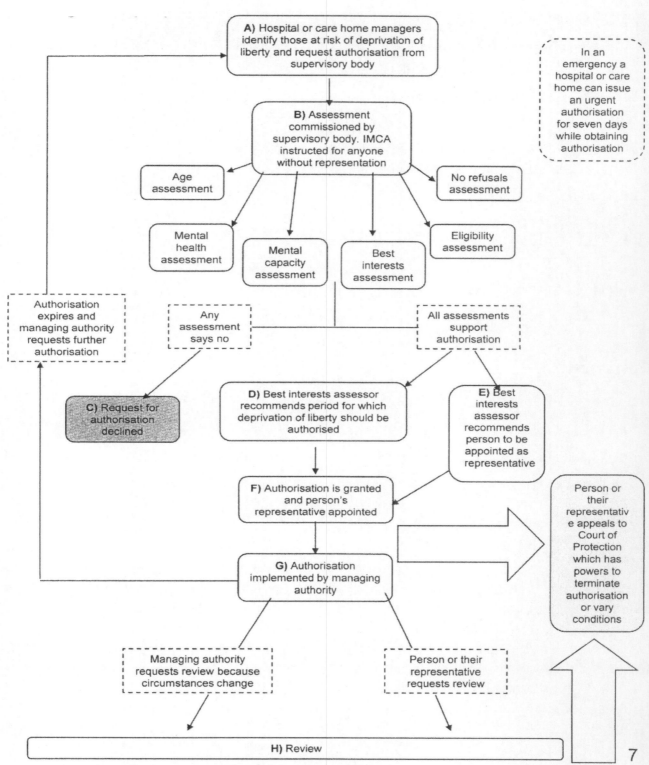

Figure 1. Overview of Deprivation of Liberty Safeguards proposals

Workbook Review

This workbook has taken you from *No Secrets* in 2000 through to the implementation of the *Mental Capacity Act 2005* in October 2007 and *Safeguarding Vulnerable Groups Act 2006.*

We have looked at the early challenges presented by *No Secrets* and at how some have been overcome but quite a few others remain.

Most of *No Secrets* has been put in place but arrangements for adult protection vary from authority to authority as:

> *No new funding has been made available.*

You may be staggered to learn that the funding for POVA is taken from the heavily under-resourced Community Care Budget which provides services for service users and carers. Certain behaviours have been criminalised under Section 44, namely:

- Wilful neglect.

- Ill treatment.

We are surprised local authorities have not turned to local:

> *Community Safety Partnerships to at least part-fund adult protection pursuits.*

We have described:

- The types of abuse.

- Mitigating and aggravating factors.

- Where abuse can occur.

- The need to respect Human Rights

- The need to ensure our practice is *balanced* to avoid errors of omission and commission in law.

We have examined the:

- Central role of capacity

- Familiarised you with the incapacity checklist

- Outlined the powers available to protect vulnerable adults including:
  – Declaratory Relief
  – Lasting Power of Attorney
  – Appointees and Deputies

– Court of Protection decisions, and
– Advance decisions

We hope this workbook will help you in your practice with vulnerable adults.

Learning Outcomes

Use this checklist to review what you have achieved from using this workbook. You will see it is an exact repeat of the Learning Profile you completed at the start. Tick the box that most nearly represents your knowledge, having now completed this workbook.

Session One

I can:

	Not at all	*Partly*	*Very well*
• Explain the origin of *No Secrets*.	☐	☐	☐
• Summarise its main objectives.	☐	☐	☐

Session Two

I can:

	Not at all	*Partly*	*Very well*
• Identify informal and formal aspects of inter-agency co-operation.	☐	☐	☐
• Explain how multi-agency teams were created, and their main purposes.	☐	☐	☐
• Explain what is meant by 'lead body' and its implications for practice.	☐	☐	☐

Session Three

I can:

	Not at all	*Partly*	*Very well*
• Identify the key stakeholders in *No Secrets*.	☐	☐	☐
• Explain the need to establish a multi-agency management committee (adult protection).	☐	☐	☐
• Explain why *No Secrets* has not been underpinned by new legislation.	☐	☐	☐

Session Four

I can:

	Not at all	Partly	Very well
• Identify where abuse is likely to take place.	☐	☐	☐
• Describe the procedures already in place for investigating certain types of abuse and complaints.	☐	☐	☐
• Pin-point gaps in current provisions to protect vulnerable adults.	☐	☐	☐

Session Five

I can:

	Not at all	Partly	Very well
• Have awareness of the challenges presented by the implementation of *No Secrets*.	☐	☐	☐
• Identify things I can contribute.	☐	☐	☐
• Confirm my understanding of the various kinds of abuse which can occur.	☐	☐	☐
• Explain the role of the multi-agency management committee and the vulnerable adults protection team.	☐	☐	☐
• Outline why investigation procedures are necessary.	☐	☐	☐

Session Six

I can:

	Not at all	Partly	Very well
• Outline the key principles underpinning effective practice.	☐	☐	☐
• Detail the key issues in assessing risk.	☐	☐	☐
• Describe the range of outcomes that can follow from an initial concern.	☐	☐	☐

Session Seven

I can:

	Not at all	Partly	Very well
• Describe the dilemmas that confront *professionals* responding to domestic violence.	☐	☐	☐

- Explain how the nature of privacy may affect my response to domestic violence. □ □ □

- Describe legal provisions to protect victims of domestic violence and which enable them to remain in their own homes. □ □ □

Session Eight

I can:

	Not at all	*Partly*	*Very well*

- Outline the principles which apply when determining capacity and describe the practical test used to determine capacity. □ □ □

- Explain the **new** provisions contained in the *Mental Capacity Act 2005*. □ □ □

- Describe the dilemmas posed by capacity and compulsion. □ □ □

Session Nine

I can:

	Not at all	*Partly*	*Very well*

- Describe the main provisions of the *Mental Capacity Act 2005*. □ □ □

- Explain how finances are protected. □ □ □

- Explain how healthcare and treatment issues are dealt with for people who lack capacity. □ □ □

- Describe what is meant by an advance decision and explain how, and when, these should be used. □ □ □

You may find it helpful to go back over the material you still feel uncertain about. On the other hand you may have found it hard to gauge your current level of understanding. If so I suggest you discuss your work with your tutor next time you meet.

Finally, if for any reason you felt that the workbook provided you with insufficient material to develop your understanding, you should refer to your tutor for further reading and guidance.

Bibliography

Biggs, S. (1997) In Ovretviet, J. (Ed.) *Inter-Professional Working for Health and Social Care.* Basingstoke: Palgrave Macmillan.

Brayne, H. and Carr, H. (2005) *Law for Social Workers.* 9th rev. edition. Oxford: OUP.

Challis, D. et al. (1994) *Case Management: A Review of UK Developments and Issues.* In Titterton, M. (Ed.) *Caring for People in the Community.* London: Jessica Kingsley.

Department of Constitutional Affairs (2007) *Mental Capacity Act 2005: Code of Practice.* London: TSO.

DoH/HO (2000) *No Secrets.* London: TSO.

DoH (1990) *Working Together Under the Children Act 1989.* London: TSO.

Dimond, B. (2004) *Legal Aspects of Health Care.* Oxford: OUP.

Hart, D. (1998) *Working Across Boundaries.* London: Open Learning Foundation.

Henderson, P. (1995) *Children and Communities.* London: Pluto Press.

HO/Lord Chancellors Office/CPS/DoH (2001) *Achieving Best Evidence in Criminal Proceedings: Guidance for Vulnerable or Intimidated Witnesses.* London: TSO.

Leveridge, M. (2007) Community Care and Care Management. In Tovey, W. (Ed.) *The Post Qualifying Handbook for Social Workers.* London: Jessica Kingsley.

Montgomery, J. (2003) *Health Care Law.* Oxford: OUP.

Payne, M. (2000) *Teamwork in Multi-professional Care.* Basingstoke: Macmillan.

Pincus, A. and Minahan, A. (1973) *Social Work Practice: Model and Method.* Itrasca, IL: F.E. Peacock.

Ranson, S. and Stewart, J. (1994) *Management for the Public Domain: Enabling the Learning Society.* London: Palgrave Macmillan.

Schwehr, B. (2002) Legal Breakthrough for Adult Protection. *Care and Health Magazine,* 18.

Taylor, M. (1997) *The Best of Both Worlds. Report for Joseph Rowntree Foundation.* York: York Publishing Services.

Tees Wide Policy and Guidance (2007) available from Middlesbrough Social Services.

Wadham, J. and Mountfield, H. (2000) *Blackstone's Guide to the Human Rights Act 1998.* Oxford: Blackstone Press.

Wren, M. (2007) Learning Disabilities Today: Integrated Working. In Tovey, W. (Ed.) *The Post Qualifying Handbook for Social Workers.* London: Jessica Kingsley.

You are also strongly advised to read the *Journal for Adult Protection* on a regular basis to keep up to date with developments.

Appendix 1
Key Provisions of Relevant Legislation

Assessment of need and risk

Section 47(1) *NHSCCA 1990* and if a disabled person, Section 47(2) also applies.

Assessment of carers

Section 47(1), *NHSCCA 1990* but as a result of the *Carers (Recognition and Services) Act 1995*.

Supporting vulnerable people giving evidence

Powers contained in the *Youth Justice and Criminal Evidence Act 1999*.

Ensuring those working with vulnerable people are fit to do so

The *Safeguarding Vulnerable Groups Act 2006* which requires everyone working with, or volunteering to work with, vulnerable people, to be registered with the Independent Safeguarding Authority.

Determination of capacity

Practical test to be found in the *Mental Capacity Act 2005* under Section 3.

Protection of finances

The *Mental Capacity Act 2005*.

Advanced decisions and IMCAs

The Mental Capacity Act 2005.

Powers to remove a person lacking capacity at risk of harm from their home

Common law Order of Declaratory Relief.

Safeguards to the removal of people who lack capacity

The *Mental Health Act 2007* which amends the *Mental Capacity Act 2005*.

Registration, inspection and maintenance of minimum standards in residential accommodation

The *Care Standards Act 2000*.

Duties given to the current Care Standards Quality Commission Inspectorate (CSCI).

Requirements for a complaints procedure

Section 50, *NHSCCA 1990*.

Legal rights to investigate

None. However, you can argue that under the *Mental Capacity Act 2005*, you are acting in the person's 'best interest'. If suspected willful neglect or ill treatment and the person lacks capacity you could investigate this as a suspected offence under Section 44, *MCA 2005*.

Protection of whistleblowers

Public Interest Disclosure Acts 1998 and *2004*.

Over-arching responsibility

You must abide by the Articles of the European Convention as adopted by the Human Rights Act 1998 and it is a criminal offence for a public body to breach any Article.

Protecting the liberty of those who lack capacity

The *Mental Health Act 2007* amends the *Mental Capacity Act 2005* to introduce new deprivation of liberty safeguards. These are contained in detail in a new supplement to the 2nd Code of Practice to the *MCA 2005*.

Appendix 2
Investigation Action Model

Abuse in the Home

If the person has capacity	If the person lacks capacity
1. Notify Safeguarding (Adult Protection).	1. Notify Safeguarding (Adult Protection).
2. Is it a crime? – If so, the police may investigate.	2. Is it a crime – If so the police may investigate.
3. Does the person want help? – If yes, carry out an investigation and act as to what is needed – If no, offer advice and suggest they contact Age Concern or a similar body for support.	3. Can the person make a decision on this matter?
	4. Does anyone have LPA?
	5. If abuse by the attorney consider a challenge at court.
4. Reassure them its OK to contact you again if the abuse recurs.	6. Does the abuser live with them?
	7. How serious is the abuse?
	8. Consider seeking, as a last resort, an Order of Declaratory Relief.

Abuse in the community

If the person has capacity	If the person lacks capacity
1. Notify Safeguarding (Adult Protection)	1. Notify Safeguarding (Adult Protection)
2. Is it a crime?	2. Is it a crime?
3. Offer advice, and if wanted, conduct a risk assessment.	3. Ascertain the relationship to the abuser and devise a strategy to prevent future abuse.
4. Get the organisation involved, e.g. a local church, to pursue their own procedures. NB They should already have them in place.	4. Ensure the abuse is only happening at that location, and as far as possible, that there are no other victims.

Abuse at a day centre or care home (applies *regardless* of capacity)

1. Notify Safeguarding (Adult Protection).

2. Inform CSCI and determine who will take the lead.

3. Is it a crime? – police may investigate.

4. Alleged abuse should be suspended pending investigation.

5. Positive steps taken to prevent future abuse.

6. If lacking capacity consider involving an IMCA to see if it is in the best interests of the vulnerable adult to change centre or care home.

7. Inform CSCI of outcome.

Updates, copying permission and electronic supply of The *Safeguarding Vulnerable Adults* Workbook

For a complete schedule of updates as they are written to address changes in law and guidance, please visit www.russellhouse.co.uk and search for 'Safeguarding Vulnerable Adults' where update information is prominently displayed. To obtain these updates, you will need to register your purchase of this manual by completing and submitting the form on pages 127 and 128.

Photocopying permission and electronic supply of the workbook

This *Safeguarding Vulnerable Adults* manual is sufficient on its own for you to start delivering training and teaching across the organisation.

But as the material covered in the workbook is subject to change over time, as a result of changes in laws, judgements and government guidance, the author aims to develop materials to help you keep your teaching and training fresh and up-to-date.

As a goal of the overall package is to improve work with vulnerable adults in both large and smaller organisations, the learning materials can be used in ways that are suitable for each.

Use of the workbook in large organisations

Large organisations, such as colleges or universities, large charities or government agencies, who regularly train many (10 or more) students and/or workers each year:

- *may not* **photocopy** the materials provided in this manual for training or teaching these students or practitioners.

Instead they can, after purchasing and paying for this manual:

- complete the form at the back of this book to **purchase a PDF version**, which they can then use with any number of learners within their organisation, electronically or by printing copies. (See *Using the electronic version of the workbook within your organisation* on page 124 for advice on how far you may use the electronic version within your organisation.) You will be supplied with the latest version, which in future years will almost certainly be somewhat different from the workbook in the manual you are reading now, reflecting changes in law, judgements and government guidance on best practice. Prepayment of £195.00 plus VAT is required before we can deliver – by email – your first PDF.

- thereby **enrol to receive notifications** from the publisher concerning updates from the author:
  - **annually** in the spring when the author aims to provide a completely updated workbook for the next year's teaching and training, available for purchase from the publisher as a PDF. The price of annual updates will be advised in the notification sent to you each year, and will change each year depending on the extent of changes, but will be something like half the price of the first PDF. You are under no obligation to purchase, but will continue to receive news and notifications even if you do not purchase an update each year (unless of course you ask us to stop sending notifications to you).
  - **occasionally, between annual updates**, with advice from the author that each organisation may wish to pass on to their current and prior students.

Use of the workbook in smaller organisations

Smaller organisations, such as small charities or care homes, and the like, can of course take advantage of exactly the same offer that is made to large organisations, as described immediately above. But, alternatively to help those on limited budgets, organisations of this type who train just a few (less than 10) students or practitioners each year, after they have bought and paid for this manual:

- *may* **photocopy** Part 2 of this manual, but only for those few learners each year.

- and complete the form at the back of this book to receive **notifications from the publisher concerning updates** from the author:
  - **annually** in the spring when the author aims to provide a completely updated workbook for the next year's teaching and training, available for purchase from the publisher as loose printed pages. The price of annual updates will be advised in the notification sent to you each year, and will change each year depending on the extent of changes, but will be something like £15 each year. You are under no obligation to purchase, but will continue to receive news and notifications even if you do not purchase an update each year (unless of course you ask us to stop sending notifications to you).
  - **occasionally, between annual updates**, with advice from the author that each organisation may wish to pass on to their current and prior students.

Use of the workbook by trainers who work with more than one organisation

Trainers who work with more than one organisation and who want to use The *Safeguarding Vulnerable Adults* Workbook should please make sure that each organisation buys a copy of the manual and registers for receipt of notification of updates. (See *Using the electronic version of the workbook within your organisation* on page 124 for advice on how far you may use the electronic version within any one organisation.)

This chart provides a quick summary of – but does not replace – the guidance given on immediately prior pages concerning copying rights, provision of material in electronic format and updates. See page 124 for advice on how far you may use the electronic version within any one organisation.

Scale and nature of usage	Photcopying	Supply of material electronically	Annual update
Large scale usage within larger organisations* (training more than 10 learners each year).	Not permitted	A PDF of the complete workbook can be purchased for £195 plus VAT.	**Annual updates** of the workbook will be offered in PDF format at a cost that is proportional to the extent of the new material. Probably about £100–125 plus VAT. **Interim updates** of news, commentary and suggestions for teaching and training will be offered at no additional cost during the currency of the annually updated subscription.
Small scale usage within* smaller organisations (training 10 or less learners each year).	Permitted for the few learners trained each year.		**Annual updates** of the work will be offered for purchase as hard copy pages at a cost that is proportional to the extent of the new material. Probably about £15–20 plus VAT. **Interim updates** of news, commentary and suggestions for teaching and training will be offered at no additional cost during the currency of the annually updated subscription.
Use in more than one organisation by trainers or teachers.	The trainer should ensure that each organisation (as detailed under **Using the electronic version of the workbook within your organisation** on page 124) purchases a copy of the manual. The organisation must then register for PDFs and updates according to their size as described above, before the trainer distributes any parts of the workbook to learners in that organisation.		

*Smaller organisations can, of course, purchase the PDF of the workbook (£195 plus VAT) and the electronic updates (about £100-125 plus VAT) in the same way as larger organisations can.

Responsible and respectful use of the copying rights and electronic materials

The guidance set out in the section *Updates, copying permission and electronic supply of The* Safeguarding Vulnerable Adults *Workbook* is based on:

- respect for the author's copyright

- the view that their work in developing carefully distilled and critical learning materials to help you improve the training of people who work with vulnerable adults deserves to be remunerated.

The publisher and author therefore seek everyone's respectful and responsible and honourable co-operation in use of their work within the terms and conditions that have already been set out.

What the complete package offers

Reciprocating this respect and responsible co-operation, the publisher and author have:

- Put in place the processes that have already been described that enable organisations to copy and digitally copy the workbook, with a minimum of fuss, for use by their learners.

- Kept the costs of obtaining these permissions at sensibly low levels by using appropriate, rather than the most sophisticated, technologies.

- Included within this suitable arrangements for both large and smaller organisations.

- Kept the introductory price of buying this initial manual well within the budgets of large and smaller organisations. Everyone with responsibility for safeguarding vulnerable adults can assess the value to them of the author's work on a free trial basis. (If you do not want to use the *Safeguarding Vulnerable Adults* package, you can return this manual in clean and resaleable condition for full credit.)

Thank you. We hope that you will find this package useful and that it helps enhance practice with vulnerable adults.

Using the electronic version of the workbook within your organisation

It has been clearly stated that:

- organisations who register their purchase of this manual and pay for the electronic version of the workbook and news updates, and perhaps then also pay separately for the annual updates, can copy the workbook in electronic or hard copy to learners across their organisation.

- trainers who work with more than one organisation and who want to use The *Safeguarding Vulnerable Adults* Workbook should please make sure that each organisation buys a copy of the manual and registers for receipt of notification of updates.

Within this guidance, by way of example, this means that the author and publisher are happy, for the workbook to be:

- used across an entire agency or department of any one local authority, for example Bassetshire Social Services.

- used across various parts of a health trust.

- used within all parts of a large charity that is constituted as a single organisation.

But it does not mean that:

- a local authority (or, indeed, national government) may register it with one of its departments and use it across more than that one department. Each department needs to register separately.

- the NHS may register it within one trust and use it across more than that one NHS trust. Each trust needs to register separately.

- one organisation may register their purchase and use the materials with learners in other agencies with whom they are in a partnership or network. Each partner or network member needs to register separately.

If you are in any doubt about how to apply these examples to your particular circumstance, you should contact the publisher, via email at help@russellhouse.co.uk. We are here to help you.

Other copying permission and restrictions

- If you have not purchased a copy of this manual: none of the permissions to copy material from this manual that are described in this manual – or to use the PDF version of it – is granted to anyone other than a purchaser of *Safeguarding Vulnerable Adults*. If in doubt, anyone wanting permission to use this material should contact the publisher, via email at help@russellhouse.co.uk.

- If you want to copy all or part of the manual in any context other than set out here in ways that go beyond normal fair trading guidelines, you should first seek permission in the usual way:
  – either via Russell House Publishing
  – or via the Copyright Licensing Agency.

- If you want to make any digital copies of all or part of this manual in any other context than set out here, you should contact Russell House Publishing, as the content of this manual is currently excluded from the digital licensing arrangements of the Copyright Licensing Agency.

If in doubt, anyone wanting to make photocopies should contact the publisher, via email at help@russellhouse.co.uk. We are here to answer your questions helpfully.

Order form for PDF of workbook
and
Registration form to receive notification of updates

Please complete the form below, tear out this page, and return it to us. Please note that photocopies are not acceptable, nor are applications made through e-mail, phone or fax. Please keep a copy of the completed form for your own records.

Anyone completing any part of this form must tick one of the following 2 boxes.

I/we have read and understood the preceding section of this manual, *Updates, Copying Permission and Electronic Supply of The* Safeguarding Vulnerable Adults *Workbook*, and agree to abide by the guidance set out there for:

☐ Use of The *Safeguarding Vulnerable Adults* Workbook in a single large organisation, training more than 10 people in a year.

☐ Use of The *Safeguarding Vulnerable Adults* Workbook in a single smaller organisation, training 10 or less people in a year

I understand that the publisher (RHP) reserves the right to qualify or reject any application which it is not completely satisfied is on an original torn-out page from the back of a purchased book.

PDF of workbook

☐ Please supply The *Safeguarding Vulnerable Adults* Workbook as a PDF at £195.00 plus

VAT = £229.12 to this email address: _____

and thereby licence me to use the PDF only in the organisation identified by me on the next page.

Anyone ordering a PDF must tick one of the following 3 boxes.

☐ I enclose payment of £195 + VAT = £229.12

☐ Please invoice me. I understand that the electronic version will be sent on receipt by RHP of payment in full.

☐ I would like to pay £195.00 + VAT = £229.12 by my credit/debit card, which is registered at the address on the next page.

☐ Visa ☐ Eurocard/Mastercard ☐ Delta ☐ Maestro – issue number _____

Start date_____ Expiry date _____

Credit card no. _____ Security code _____

Signed _____

Registration for updates

To obtain updates, please tick one of the following 2 boxes.

☐ I/we have ordered a PDF of The *Safeguarding Vulnerable Adults* Workbook. As soon as I have paid for it, please start sending notifications of opportunities to purchase **complete annual updates of the PDF and interim updating news** to the email address provided below.

☐ I/we have **not** ordered a PDF and have ticked the '**small organisation box**' on this form. Please start sending me notifications of opportunities to purchase **complete annual updates as printed loose sheets and interim updating news** to the email address provided below.

NOTE: The author and publisher will make every effort to provide notification of updates in a timely fashion, but no contractual relationship between purchaser and publisher exists beyond the supply of the material that has been paid for.

Anyone completing any part of this form must fill in, sign and date the following section.

Name _____

Organisation _____

Address _____

_____

_____

_____

Post code _____

Contact phone number _____

E-mail _____

I understand that RHP may use this information to contact me about other matters and publications, but that RHP will not make my details available to other organisations.

Signed: _____   Date _____

Please return this form to:

Russell House Publishing Ltd, 3 St George's House, Uplyme Road Business Park, Lyme Regis, Dorset DT7 3LS.

RHP reserves the right to withdraw this offer and/or change this price at any time without prior notice.